BODY LANGUAGE

****

Learn how to analyze and read people through the body language and use of powerful communication to influence them

By: Oliver Peterson

reparation, damages, or monetary loss due to the information herein, either directly or indirectly.

Respective authors own all copyrights not held by the publisher.

The information herein is offered for informational purposes solely and is universal as so. The presentation of the information is without a contract or any guarantee assurance.

The trademarks that are used are without any consent, and the publication of the trademark is without permission or backing by the trademark owner. All trademarks and brands within this book are for clarifying purposes only and are owned by the owners themselves, not affiliated with this document.

ABOUT THE BOOK

Have you ever thought about how well you can read other people's body language? The fact is that what people say is sometimes different from what they think or feel. It works the other way too. Your body language influences what others think of you, so you don't want to send the wrong signals.

We all use body language gestures to reinforce what we say and how we feel. Regardless of whether the posture is conscious or involuntary, it tends to support the strengths (and weaknesses) of our personality. Therefore, it is essential to remember that others, while reading body language, also consciously and unconsciously read our body language cues.

Many of the feelings we have when judging people are an evaluation of the person on a subconscious level. The way we interpret a person's body language plays a vital role in the opinions we make about others. If you ever wondered why you distrust someone you don't know, there is probably something in that person's body language with the red flag.

Even if we use voluntary gestures while communicating with others, we should only use body language that feels natural. You don't want to turn to others as if you were rehearsing the conversation. Any conscious effort that invests in your body language should be to avoid gestures that can send negative messages about your personality. The good news is that proper body language automatically established when we try to be ourselves. The key is to be safe and relaxed. When you feel comfortable, other people probably feel comfortable in your presence.

People who send positive signals for body language run with their heads and shoulders raised. Honesty is a sign of trust. People tend to trust you to keep in touch during a conversation or discussion. While walking or sitting, keep your arms at your sides and palms open. Other people generally interpret this attitude as a sign that you are accessible and that they can trust you.

Be careful not to adopt an indifferent or defensive attitude when you meet someone for the first time. When you feel more secure, when you stop in a certain way, you adopt the position that is comfortable for you and you look safer. You want to try to look bigger by occupying more space around you. This will make you safer and essential to others.

Giving people a real smile is one of the best ways to feel comfortable in their presence. However, they want this smile to spread across your lips, so they believe it is sincere. A warm smile helps calm other people. If your smile seems nervous, it will probably also make other people nervous. If you shake hands with someone, the handshake should be firm and not weak. He wants people to receive the message that he is safe and sincere. However, be careful not to over-tighten a person's hand; otherwise, it will give you the impression of having an aggressive personality. While you want to be sure of yourself, you don't want to be bossy or dominant.

You should also make sure you are welcome before you get so close to a person's personal space. This is easier if you already know the person. When we meet people, we begin to internalize many of their common body language patterns. Once we are familiar with the normal behavior of another person, we can better observe the mood or attitude changes of that person.

The way you breathe can also demonstrate positive body language. If you breathe slowly and deeply, you may feel less anxious. This is highly important, especially if you are with someone you met for the first time. Instead of looking nervous and tense, you should be calm and relaxed. Calm breathing releases tension.

If you want to learn more about body language, then this book is for you.

Table of Contents

INTRODUCTION

Body language is the manner of communicating what you are thinking or feeling by the way you carry and move your body rather than by words. It is the

unspoken or non-verbal mode of communication that we do in every single aspect of our interaction with people and hugely responsible for the impressions we create in people's minds about our personality.

Statistically, about 60%-80% of what we really mean is communicated through the non-verbal language which is transmitted through our body language (with voice tonality contributing about 38%) and that the actual verbal communication through words, accounts for just 7% - 10%.

The main impression we build in people's mind about us is the strongest and utmost lasting because it takes almost two to four minutes for most people to come to a choice of likability for an individual.

Our use and reading of body language is mostly an unconscious process we carry out in our daily lives. Therefore, our ability to use body language positively and the ability to read other people's mind through their body languages can help us develop a better overall personality.

Women are naturally considered to be ten times better than average men at being able to read and communicate with subtle body language. They can generally tell a person's mood just by looking and detect all kinds of things from body language.

Literally speaking, in the dating game, women generally use their heads, and men use their chests in most of their non-verbal communication. The women toss their hair or sweep their heads backs as signs of attraction while the men would simply puff out their chests, walking upright, holding their head up and their shoulders back. Also, the female will often have an accentuated roll of the hips while walking near the object of her interest.

The art of reading body language is anything but an exact science. It is part of the observation, two parts of the interpretation. Look for consistent groups of gestures, sudden incoherent movement, and patterns. You have to read a lot of body language in groups instead of forming a firm opinion of action. Sometimes it is easier for an external observer to understand the characters than for the actual participant.

Body language is another term for nonverbal communication we have with our bodies every day. Eighty percent of our daily communication is considered nonverbal. The research on body language can be made manifest by studying a series of body gestures, enlarging the eyes and even changing the tone of our voice in a specific circumstance.

The specific basis of body language is that the limbic system of our body, the reptilian brain that controls our most basic survival functions, includes combat or evasion response, naturally invites our bodies to perform certain gestures. Even children seem to intuitively know how body language works and can communicate their needs through their small body gestures. Children learn at an early age how certain gestures produce specific reactions. For example, a slight smile and bowing of the head often lead to increased attention. Even the "yes" and "no" tremor seems to come from our childhood when the "yes" nodded allowed us to find our mother's breast from which we can feed, and the "no" bowed. The power supply has finished the process.

When we are children, the signs of body language are more evident because we have not learned to hide them or minimize them. As a result, children are excellent examples of learning when it comes to non-verbal communication. Children generally have little control over their responses to different situations. So if they like something or don't like it, they usually let them know. As a result, a more natural limbic body language is observed in children than in adults. For example, when a child lies, it tends to cover itself or touch its mouth, almost to prevent the lie from escaping. As we age, we could distract this movement by scratching our nose or combing our fingers through our hair.

With age, we learn to mask our faces and some of our movements. In these cases, body language examines the parts of the body on which we have little or no control and the parts of the body that we generally ignore. This means observing our feet, the dilation of the pupils, and the tone of our voices. Our feet are one of the few parts of the body that really don't matter to us unless we consciously think about it. As a result, people who learn body language often start to stand. They can tell you who the dominant person in the relationship is, if someone is really interested in you and if someone is ready to start.

Pupil dilation is another sign of body language that is observed to determine if someone likes or dislikes something. This reaction, however, is only temporary. If you are not close enough to observe your original response to a visual stimulus, you will lose pupil dilation. We must also be aware of our tone of voice, as our voice often reflects the emotions we experience. For example, if many items are emphasized, the tone will increase. If a person's tone doesn't change, if he says something to which an emotional reaction must be connected, it can be a sign of fraud.

Negative sign of body language

Displaying one of the following signals may be a warning signal in the absence of interest.

1. Arms crossed. Any type of defensive posture indicates a barrier between two people when they speak.

2. Remove your body or leave no room for minimal body contact. When you are no longer interested in someone, try to get away and decrease contact and most forms of connection between the parties.

3. Lack of attention to what you say.

4. Lack of eye contact and look away from the eyes. Runaway eyes and blinking eyes may indicate deception.

5. Frequent assent indicates a loss of connection most of the time.

6. Yawning can usually indicate a state of boredom and is a sure sign of lack of interest.

Positive signs of body language.

The following are good indicators of the interest shown by your partner.

1. High eye contact and flickering. When one person likes another, he usually tries to adapt and stay in sync with the other, which is fun and increases the attraction between them. Intense flirting often causes eye contact with the eyes, as well as a long, hard look in the mouth.

2. Nodding a small nod is a good signal if it is made periodically to indicate that you are at the same wavelength.

3. Increased physical contact. If the contact is warm instead of suggestive, there is progress.

4. It is a good sign of interest to lean the body forward and keep it in a relaxed position pointing towards the attractive person. These break the barriers,

indicating an open and non-defensive, relaxed and comfortable mind.

5. Mirror and unconsciously reflect each other's behavior: lean forward at the same time, breathe in sync, cross the same leg at the same time, and speak in the same tone means that it is a certain attraction since that implies both at the same level of attraction.

CHAPTER 1

BODY LANGUAGE

One of the most influential communication methods we use in our daily interactions is our non-verbal or body language. It is the kind of communication that ignites the emotions and reactions of our "intestinal level." Research has shown that understanding body language increases your ability to achieve anything you want in a given situation.

Have you ever seen a couple sitting together and understanding in minutes how good or bad their relationship was? Have you ever thought of how you managed to achieve this result so quickly without direct rapport? Maybe you know it or not, we spend our days responding to the non-verbal signals of people projected through their body language and drawing conclusions from our observations.

Our body language reveals the truth that we hide from the world in our words; it makes us realize how we feel about ourselves, our relationships and our situations. Through eye contact, gestures, posture, and facial expressions, the people we interact with can determine our intentions, the quality of our relationships, our ability in every situation, our trust and our true motivations and desires.

The power of body language lies in the emotional response it creates. Feelings guide decisions and reactions in almost every situation. Nonverbal cues trigger feelings that determine the basic resources of an individual, such as truth, reliability, sincerity, level of competence, and leadership qualities. The interpretation of these ideas can determine who we are, what work we are responsible for, what we achieve and who can be chosen in influential political positions.

We could spend years learning and developing effective body language skills with such an important skill. The fact is that most people underestimate the importance of body language until they seek a better understanding of human behavior in a personal relationship or gain an advantage in a highly competitive business situation.

The mastery of body language allows people to interpret the meaning behind certain gestures and body movements and to understand how messages can be projected and effectively communicated when dealing with others. As a result, the overall effectiveness of interpersonal relationships has increased considerably. The best way to begin this mastery process is to learn the basic interpretation of the two main types of body language: open presence and closed presence.

The type of closed spoken body language is described in people who bend the body around the midline of the body, which extends from the top of the head to the feet directly towards the center of the body. The physical qualities that create this type of presence are the feet very close together, the arms close to the body, the hands crossed or joined in front of the body, the small movements of the hands, the shoulders forward and the eyes, concentrated at eye level.

The messages that are sent to the world through the closed nature of the presence of body language are lack of confidence, low self-esteem, helplessness, and lack of experience. In extreme cases, you can even generate the message of wanting to be invisible. The impact on the person who projects this type of body language can vary from the fact that he does not get the best possible opportunity, to the worst scenario of a vision of self-fulfilling victimization.

On the contrary, the open presence is represented by individuals who create a sense of authority, power, and leadership by projecting confidence, success, strength, and mastery of skills. The physical characteristics are the feet widely separated from the hips, the movements of the open hands used in conversations outside the central line of the body, the elbows away from the body, the shoulders retained, the straight positions and the eyes focused at the height of the eyes. These people consider themselves attractive, successful, intelligent, and seem to succeed without any problem. We consider this type of body language as the "body language of the leader."

To improve body language and project an open presence, eye contact is the key. Eye interaction is one of the most vital means of communication. Using direct eye contact while interacting with others can change the way people see them. When people begin to speak directly in the eyes of a person, they are considered safe, reliable, and capable.

Hand gestures and facial expressions are the second levels of change that can be visualized with an open presence. These communication methods are ideal for improving the ability to communicate clearly and effectively. The skillful use of open hand movements and the expressive effect of the face produce a greater impact when speaking, visually stimulating the listener and increasing the amount of information provided during the interaction.

Even when we are children, they teach us that good children are sitting correctly, with their legs together and hands crossed in front of them. The stimulus to limit physical space, such as children, can produce some of the characteristics found in the body language of adult presence. To counteract this effect, one can begin to assume the characteristics of the open presence body language and integrate those paths into their natural state of being. Upon completing this change in behavior, the same impressions, and nonverbal messages as the open presence counterparts will be displayed. We could spend years learning and developing effective body language skills with such an important skill. The fact is that most people underestimate the importance of body language until they seek a better understanding of human behavior in a personal relationship or gain an advantage in a highly competitive business situation.

The mastery of body language allows people to interpret the meaning behind certain gestures and body movements and to understand how messages can be projected and effectively communicated when dealing with others. As a result, the overall effectiveness of interpersonal relationships has increased considerably. The best way to begin this mastery process is to learn the basic interpretation of the two main types of body language: open presence and closed presence.

The type of closed spoken body language is described in people who bend the body around the midline of the body, which extends from the top of the head to the feet directly towards the center of the body. The physical qualities that create this type of presence are the feet very close together, the arms close to the body, the hands crossed or joined in front of the body, the small movements of the hands, the shoulders forward and the eyes — concentrated at eye level.

The messages that are sent to the world through the closed nature of the presence of body language are lack of confidence, low self-esteem, helplessness, and lack of experience. In extreme cases, you can even generate the message of wanting to be invisible. The impact on the person who projects this type of body language can vary from the fact that he does not get the best possible opportunity, to the worst scenario of a vision of self-fulfilling victimization.

Mastery of body language is crucial to create the most effective presence in all interpersonal interactions. People without this domain tend to be misunderstood and try to communicate their ideas without success. With the ability to distinguish between different modes of body language, anyone can gain the necessary mastery to succeed in any effort they choose.

Communication is one of the most significant things we do in life. Due to its many characteristics, it is also very liable to misinterpreted. However, it is good to have as much awareness as possible, not only to be; otherwise, but also to understand others more clearly. Unfortunately, some of the most powerful aspects of communication are often not consciously recognized, not to talk of being used with mastery. Furthermore, they also fall into the category of body language. In my witness service, I saw unnecessarily catastrophic results with inadequately prepared witnesses regarding behavior or body language.

Many of us don't realize the unintentional messages we send. Whether with family, friends, opponents, colleagues, speakers, or legal statements, it is helpful to know what we send every minute. Even when we tend to be silent, our body language still transmits. And when we speak, our true words are only part of the message. The rest we recorded is in our tone. Many mothers were warned to warn: "Don't use that tone with me!"

In the late 1800s, the now-legendary Charles Darwin wrote the expression of feelings in man and animal. This was the first known scientific research on what is known as body language (including nonverbal communication) and behavior, which is often known as "behavior" in humans. Subsequently, the types, expressions, and effects of communication and spoken and non-spoken behavior were examined in detail. While these signs are often so subtle that we don't know them, research has identified a great variety. Unlike Darwin, in this book, we focus exclusively on humanity. However, with the disgust of humanity, it is worth noting that animals in tonal and nonverbal communication seem much more skilled than many of us humans.

What does body language mean, and how do we recognize it? Does having your arms crossed only suggests that someone is protecting themselves or blocking others from getting too close, as is the general assumption? Would it also mean that the person is physically uncomfortable, such as cold or pain? Could it mean that I could be scared? Or possibly angry? And what about changing the eyes or not establishing eye contact? These are often perceived as indicative of dishonesty. However, what happens if the person is really shy? Maybe confused? Or even scared?

As the fields of personal growth and psychology became popular since the 1970s, research on body language has grown significantly. However, after the publication of Julius Fast's acclaimed book, body language, public media and even some of the so-called "experts" still, focus on the overly simplified interpretation of seemingly defensive postures such as crossing arms and crossing legs. While these nonverbal behaviors may indicate certain feelings and attitudes, research clearly shows that body language is much more subtle, multifaceted, and less definitive than originally recognized.

Body language and tone of voice often carry more information that leads to interpretation (or misinterpretation) than words. Therefore, it makes sense to understand, recognize, and express this as clearly as possible.

In part, body language refers to nonverbal cues that we often use unconsciously. They constitute a large percentage of our communication (or lack of communication); from facial expressions to movements and body positions, to what we don't say or how we say something. Not realizing what we are transmitting or what someone else is saying through body language and tone of voice deprives us of understanding and understanding, and perhaps even greater enjoyment of life.

What does body language mean, and how do we recognize it? Does having your arms crossed only suggests that someone is protecting themselves or blocking others from getting too close, as is the general assumption? Would it also mean that the person is physically uncomfortable, such as cold or pain? Could it mean that I could be scared? Or possibly angry? And what about changing the eyes or not establishing eye contact? These are often perceived as indicative of dishonesty. However, what happens if the person is really shy? Maybe confused? Or even scared?

As the fields of personal growth and psychology became popular since the 1970s, research on body language has grown significantly. However, after the publication of Julius Fast's acclaimed book, body language, public media and even some of the so-called "experts" still, focus on the overly simplified interpretation of seemingly defensive postures such as crossing arms and crossing legs. While these nonverbal behaviors may indicate certain feelings and attitudes, research clearly shows that body language is much more subtle, multifaceted, and less definitive than originally recognized.

Body language and tone of voice often carry more information that leads to interpretation (or misinterpretation) than words. Therefore, it makes sense to understand, recognize, and express this as clearly as possible.

In part, body language refers to nonverbal cues that we often use unconsciously. They constitute a large percentage of our communication (or lack of communication); from facial expressions to movements and body positions, to what we don't say or how we say something. Not realizing what we are transmitting or what someone else is saying through body language and tone of voice deprives us of understanding and understanding, and perhaps even greater enjoyment of life.

Luckily we can always improve. Learning to interpret and communicate better without words and to say something is an excellent way to promote the understanding of others and deliver our message more effectively. Find below some information to keep in mind:

1. Mimic is generally the most important at the beginning. Look at the various pieces of information with a frown or disapproval, clenched teeth, a radiant smile or the search for a painful face. All we have to do is turn on the television with the sound off, and no matter where

in the world, expressions of happiness, tenderness, sadness, pain, anger, and fear are universal and easy to perceive.

2. Appearance is another essential nonverbal behavior. Observing or avoiding looking, fixing, or looking the other way has important messages. Even the often unconscious flicker has social implications. Studies have shown that the flicker rate increases when people meet another person or things they love, and students expand. Alternatively, a look at someone and a very rare blink can mean aggression or, on the contrary, attract attention. Actors with a large presence on the screen often glimpse, since they rarely blink slowly. The different implications are in the associated facial muscles. A look at another person can indicate a variety of emotions, including hostility, interest, and attraction.

3. Gestures such as shaking, pointing, and using fingers and signals are important means of conveying meaning. Strength and/ or flow, as we use our arms, hands, and fingers, strongly suggest: from dancing to stress, from attempts at inclusion and peace to the attitude of hostility. The soft caress of another

person's forehead attracts attention, while a clenched fist conveys a very different message.

4. The parallelism refers to the oral communication that accompanies the words that are spoken. This includes voice, volume, inflection, meter, and tone tones. When you say something in a somewhat powerful tone, the public can interpret your approval and enthusiasm. Something that is said more violently or very silently can easily mean difficulties or even threats. The same words pronounced with a hesitant tone may indicate confusion, lack of confidence, disapproval or lack of interest. An elevator at the end transmits a very different message, as with a question.

5. Attitude can convey a lot of information. Depending on the configuration, the inclination can be interpreted in different ways. In a meeting, this can convey informal relaxation or disrespect. In a courtroom, it usually looks like the latter. Prevention can indicate interest and enthusiasm or aggression and intimidation. The rigid military march may indicate a lack of sensitivity.

6. Proxemic is one of the most subtle but very skilled aspects of body language. It refers to the space around us, which we can expect in different circumstances. People frequently refer to their need for "personal space." The volume of space we need and the amount of space we feel we belong to are subjective by several factors, including social norms, situational factors (such as driving in the subway), personality traits and name recognition. For instance, the extent of personal space desired to have an informal discussion with another person varies between 18 inches and four or five feet. When we are not at a crowded party or in an elevator, it is generally considered invasive for someone we do not know to come within 10 inches of us. Intimate conversations have an acceptable space of 0 to 12 inches or more. On the other hand, when speaking with a crowd, the estimated distance is about 2 to 3 meters, subject on the size of the audience and the place.

7. Touching or "haptic" is another key element of nonverbal behavior. Much of the research has concentrated on the importance of touch for the development

of early childhood and childhood behavior. The well-known study of Harry Harlow's monkeys showed how contact and contact withdrawal hinders complete and healthy development. Monkeys raised by nervous mothers showed persistent deficits in behavior and interaction. The same has been observed in infants and human children. The withdrawal of the intimate touch leads to degrees of separation. When we observe how people touch each other, this gives us many clues that we should keep in mind.

8. Appearance is how we want to present ourselves; if we care little or a lot is still communicating. Colors, clothing styles, ornaments or lack of ornaments, the way we use our hair and other factors that affect our appearance, create signals that people refer to. Wearing jeans for a formal event or a courtroom has a different message than what is displayed in the local cafeteria. Studies on color psychology show that different colors can influence different moods and reactions depending on society. Appearance can also influence physiological reactions, judgments, and interpretations. Consider the appearance of pop stars compared to news presenters.

Language is a gift in its diverse and rich forms. It is good to take the time to observe and practice the behavior, including vocal sounds and nonverbal body language. Of course, the information is only a beginning. The consistent application allows the domain. It is the difference between theory and practice.

Keep in mind that many signs must be taken into account to understand the body language of others better. In occasional circumstances, and if done diplomatically, the determination of the accuracy of an interpretation can be supported by reviewing our perception with the other party. Working with him can be entertaining and interesting. This awareness and ability can help anyone learn to read other people more reliably and improve our ability to communicate more effectively. It can even enrich our lives.

CHAPTER 2

BODY LANGUAGE OF PERSONS INTERPRETED

Learning to interpret body language is a very suitable ability when it comes to dealing with people. Movements are part of human communication. Subconscious movements represent 93% of human communication. The speech is only 7%. You can guess someone thinking process or mood if he knows how to interpret body language. These actions are usually unconscious. They can be a response to a situation or a biological reaction. Facial gestures, hand movements, and posture are ordered in kinetics, the learning of human movements in a statement.

These physical expressions are used to support or refer to a statement of awareness. Talking to people, there are signs to watch out for. These characters may indicate a negative setting. These negative reactions can be perceived as unpleasant if the person being analyzed is not true or has no interest. Attention should be paid to body language gestures, such as eye position, posture and hand movements. Much of eye contact and the absence of this can mean ailments. Too much attention can indicate a lack of trust. This lack of trust allows the person to pay full attention. Leaning also means distrust. This action means that the person wants to get away. Scratching the jaw or touching the earlobes is a sign of disbelief.

Body language is also used to indicate a level of comfort and intimacy. A distance of eight feet or more indicates a public distance. This type of disposal is used in public functions, e.g., to watch a movie or listen to a conference. It can be used in large groups of observers. Four to eight feet denote a social distance. Newly introduced people maintain this distance. Close enough to make contacts, but not too close to mark associations. Friends are a meter and a half away. This means a level of trust. The shortest distances that these are reserved for people close to the individual. Family, close friends and lovers are allowed on this route. This area of proximity means intimacy and a higher level of trust.

These are some of the signs you should keep in mind when talking with another person. It's easy to lie or be honest, so never trust words alone. You can use your understanding of body language to your advantage and succeed in your career, in your relationships, and in all kinds of activities in which you interact with people.

Body language is what we call a nonverbal or tacit way of communicating and interacting with another person. Being gestures, gestures, and other physical signs, body language is like a mirror that informs us about the thoughts and feelings of the other person in response to our words and actions.

In case you think that learning to read and use body language is not so important, let me show the actual statistics of the messages we receive from someone when we meet.

* 8% of the information we receive comes from what they really say.

* 37% of the information we receive comes from the tone of voice, inflection, and speed of your voice.

* The incredible 55% of the information we receive comes from your body language.

Imagine that you could leave a great impression of work, business, and love by having the knowledge and ability to read other people's thoughts. It is a very powerful tool for a successful life and general personality development.

Remember that it is equally important to send the correct signals and eliminate the incorrect signals from your own body, as this is very useful for reading other people's body language.

Keep in mind that many signals have different meanings depending on the individual and the scenario. Always look for 3 or 4 signals that contain the same message or the inconsistent signal at once. Remember, when evaluating these signals. Below are some of the common body language cues.

Body language signals:

Darting Eyes:

* Scam

* Lying down

* Trap

* Doesn't look you in the eye

* Dishonest

* Cheat

* Lack of trust

Displaced eyes:

* Scam

* Lack of trust

* Look into the eyes without looking:

* Self-confident

* Insurance

Rigid:

* Signs of aggression

* In spite of

Extended students:

* Show great interest

* Centered

* About drugs

* Feeling insecure

* Nervous

Run your fingers through your hair:

* Cleaning

* Frustration

Drumming fingers:

* Thought

* Impatient

Stand up:

* Insurance

* Show respect

Contracted

posture:

* Low self-esteem

* Low confidence

* Boring

* Feel ashamed

* Show interest in another

person Strong tremor of the

legs:

* Nervousness

* Conception

* Enthusiasm

* Aggression

* Antagonize another person

* Point the finger at another person:

* Domain

* Aggression

* Authoritarianism

High flicker rate:

* Nervousness

* Qualification

* Pluck:

* Possible hoax

* Indecision

* Bored by the current situation
  or conversation

* Think about other things

* Go to

* Aggression

* Very tense

* Challenging or triumphant

  Crossed arms:

* Defensiveness

* Closed mind

* Possible rejection

Open arms:

* Accessible

* Feels potentially vulnerable

* Open hands:

* Open heart

* Defenses below

The ability to read the signals of others is a sure way to communicate effectively. By observing how people move and gesture, you can directly address their emotions. You can see the intensity of a person's feelings through their attitude. You can see the type of mood of the other person by the speed of their gestures. When you have an idea of a person's emotions, you can respond appropriately to situations, since you are prevented and prepared for what happens next.

Take fifteen to twenty minutes a day to study and observe other people's gestures and realize their own gestures. A great learning environment is everywhere where many people meet and interact. One of the best places to observe human gestures will be an airport where people openly express enthusiasm, anger, grief, happiness, impatience, and many other emotions through gestures. Other great places include social events, business meetings, and parties.

Another excellent way to learn nonverbal communication is to watch television. Turn down the volume and try to understand what is happening by looking at the image alone without looking at the subtitles. If you increase the volume every five minutes, you can check how accurate your nonverbal readings are, and soon you can watch a complete program without sound or subtitles, and see exactly what happens to the deaf.

CHAPTER 3

COMMON LANGUAGE OF THE BODY TO AVOID

Many people use body language to send messages to their neighbors. Body language can affirm to others whenever we are happy, sad, angry, disgusted, silly, flirtatious and more. However, body language can sometimes send an incorrect message. When you meet new people, it is important to present the correct messages with your body language. This means that you know your body language with a certain degree of accuracy. Consider some common speech disorders.

Reading body language poorly is a well-known mistake, and most of us are victim of at one time or the other. Let's have a look at this illustration, the young man leaning against the wall of the supermarket, with his leg bent back and his foot propped against the wall. He wears a large, thick coat and seems out of place as if he did not belong there. As it happens, he interprets his body language as a moron, unemployed and wasting his time. But you don't think he's waiting to be taken to work. You just misunderstood this young man's body language and misunderstood his behavior. Now let's look at your body language and how people could misunderstand you.

As we have all heard, the eyes are the windows of the soul, and eye contact can send an incorrect message about you if it is not used while listening or speaking. Most people perceive the lack of eye contact as a form of disinterest. Even if you are interested in the other person, that person who is speaking can misunderstand you and end the meeting and conversation. Another common mistake in body language is to cross your arms or place something in front of you, such as a book, a chair or another object. For some people, crossing their arms or placing something in front of you sends the message that you are inaccessible because you have placed a barrier in front of you.

Some men cross their arms when they talk to another without really knowing that this is the case. We have all seen a self-confident man do this when he hears us or speaks with another person or us. Their conversation and attitude are pleasant, but those arms crossed. What do you say; Silly and immature is another form of body language, but it has its time and place. Having fun and hanging out with good and well-established friends in the park can be an acceptable time and an acceptable place to hang out. But if you are in a social function and are trying to meet new people, certainly, this is not the time for this type of nonverbal communication. If you meet new people, it may be beneficial to show your humorous side, but if you become silly, you probably won't attract new people. In fact, you may receive looks of disgust from those around you.

An incorrect attitude is a common mistake. Crouch down and for women crossed legs can like

Not smiling at new contacts is a sure way to dissuade people. It is a guaranteed way to make people avoid it, even if it doesn't really matter to you. If you don't smile, people will perceive you as inaccessible. So smile and win some friends! Now you know the most common mistakes in body language to avoid. You have a lot to laugh at!

Have you ever feel in a way whereby you were almost sure that the person you spoke with lied to you? You wanted to believe the words that came out of his mouth, but your gut said something was wrong. His eye movement, facial expressions, and body movement simply did not reflect his verbal communication. Her body language, known as nonverbal communication, had betrayed her, although they thought she had been deceived.

The capability to understand a person's body language can be a great advantage to you. Can you imagine communicating with someone and understanding what kind of message you are trying to convey before opening your mouth to say a single word? If you go one step further, what would happen if you could use your own body language to convey your message even before beginning verbal communication? If at first glance you are sending messages in body language such as "I am sure," "I am interested," "I am bored", "I am not interested," you can save a lot of time and problems.

Many communications experts believe that 50-70% of all communication is nonverbal. Just when we stop, sit down, talk and walk, everyone says something about us and reflects what really happens inside. Remember that there is not a single expression in body language that gives you a complete understanding of a person's message or situation. Everyone has their own body language. Do not jump to conclusions immediately. You are not clairvoyant!

With this in mind, you can create some common detectors for later analysis so you can infer what communication in body language someone shows you. For example, if someone lies to you, he could:

- Try to avoid eye contact by looking the other way and avoiding complete eye contact or making rapid eye movements to and from you.
- Rinse your throat frequently or change your tone of voice.
- Increase respiratory rate.
- The color of your face or neck turns red.
- Annoying, like the constant change in the movement of the foot, which shows that they are uncomfortable.
- Excessive flash.
- Offer a fake smile, no expression in your eyes.
- Avoid answering a direct question (politicians have perfected this question).

These are all signs that someone is lying to you, but as mentioned earlier, don't jump too fast to any conclusions. It could be your character to avoid eye contact or restlessness. They can be shy and insecure and feel uncomfortable while they are together.

CHAPTER 4

ATTRACTION OF BODY READING LANGUAGE

When it comes to taking love interests, sometimes the other sex just doesn't understand. Don't be frustrated; just try some simple and effective body language

tricks. Everyone uses body language all the time. We can say that we are happy, confused, disturbed or interested! But knowing what your body says is especially important when it comes to love interests. These body language indicators put your unexpressed communication skills into shape.

Occasionally lick your lips to draw attention to these beautiful wrinkles. You should use this very rarely, but occasionally lick your lips to draw attention to one of the sexiest parts of your body and show that you are interested.

Synchronize with your love interest. Being physically synchronized with someone indicates that you are also synchronized with him spiritually. Imitate some of their movements, for example. For example, drink your drink or bow down when they do. Don't overdo that. You are not supposed to be a literal mirror; you are just trying to suggest to your subconscious that both are in tune. Moving towards someone is another sign that you care about him. When you touch or rely on a love interest in your arm, your desire to be closer mentally and physically becomes evident.

Make latent eye contact. When you look at this strange seducer, you know that you are dressed. But this should not be a second class competition. Just give them the look that is long enough so they can look at them. The sexy look also works closely. If you two are already talking, make sure they know they have your full attention. You don't have to look at them, you don't have to look around each time or check the door when it opens. It's a way to show them that you care and what they say.

The flirting tips quickly capture a man's attention. If you occasionally remove your hair from your face or throw it away, you can attract great flirtatious attention in an excellent way. Another great trick is to slightly bow your head when you hit it. If you give them that look, you'll be fascinated and interested.

Place your body in your direction. Center your shoulders on the person you are interested in. When you sit and cross your legs, showing the knee sends them the same signal. It says "I am interested in you and you have my attention."

Touch or caress an object in front of you. Be sure to keep this underestimated. Slightly stroking your wine glass or touching your leg while sitting is a sign that you want to touch the person in front of you.

Would you like to show that you are interested in someone? Let your body say everything. Body language can make things happen to someone you just met or turn a friend into a love interest. If you use body language, you can say that you are interested without having to say anything.

We are often attracted to people with a good personality. A good personality shows the confidence in you that attract other people. In public, our body language plays an important role in the impression of the audience. The biggest challenge in public speaking is maintaining an effective attitude that results from good emotional intelligence. The way we deliver our speech consists of two components: visual and verbal. I think the visual component is usually more important for viewers. This mainly includes body language, posture, eye contact and facial expression of a person. More than half of his impact as a speaker depends on his body language. Can you control the words you say, have control over what you say with your body language?

Body language includes gestures, postures and facial expressions. When you speak with a large audience, all eyes are on you, so it is important to have good body language at all times. In public, your positive body language helps you build a reputation for the audience. It also helps your listeners to focus on you and what you say.

Verbal expression means using the right words

Look energetic and confident while sitting. Sitting straight in your chair, with your back straight, your feet flat on the floor and your hands open on the table makes you feel comfortable.

Avoid an exaggerated expression that can confuse the public.

Get up and introduce yourself to the audience. It is important to keep your hands at your sides or keep them carefully on the podium. Facilitate these projects.

Do not hesitate on the podium as this can distract even the most interested audience.

Avoid being behind the music stand, as it separates you from the audience while you want to bring it closer.

The height should be adjusted according to your needs.

Look at each part of the room. From right to left, from front to back, to interest each person in the audience.

Use your hands to underline a point and lessen pressure.

Do not keep your hands on your back or in your pockets. This shows nervousness.

If you cross your arms, you are not interested in communication.

No matter how much you speak in public, but if you prowl, you will surely leave the worst impression on the audience.

Keep your head up with your chin up. The chin augmentation allows you have the feeling of being in control.

Measure your gestures according to the size of the room.

Their movements must be wide and fluid, not rushed or abrupt.

The feet should point forward. If you don't gesture, your hands should sit silently at your sides.

You can move, but remember to intervene with silence from time to time.

Try to freeze your face from the beginning. Smile during the audience greeting and at other times during the speech.

Sometimes, short-lived spokesmen decide to move forward and be closer to the audience rather than clinging to the music stand to appear tall.

In fact, it is difficult for most people to be alone in front of a group of people. It is something strange that creates anxiety, tension and butterflies in the stomach. Being natural is not the abbreviation of it. We have to make an extra effort and use all our speech and presentation skills to be more expressive and influential. It is worth recharging the batteries, as this depends largely on our body language. Work on your body language to make you have the opportunity to speak in public and stand out. If you have adequate body language, proper movements, eye contact, gestures, and posture, you are on your way to public speaking successfully.

CHAPTER 5

THE ROLE OF EYE CONTACT IN BODY LANGUAGE SUIT

Eye contact is an important part of the attraction to body language. Our eyes can convey a variety of emotions, such as shock, anger, sexuality and more.

In many cases, this is the first sign that two strangers are attracted to each other.

A woman looks at a man on the other side of the place. He also recognizes the woman and starts looking at her. She blushes and quickly walks away in an instant, as she is shy and eager to show interest. After a few seconds, she looks back. He still looks and smiles. She takes the courage to look forward and smiles back.

Slowly, he crosses the room to meet her and find out more about her.

Or a sign of body language of lifelong friends.

Two people are sitting at the table, having fun with each other's company and rarely make eye contact. This means they feel very comfortable and share a clear sense of trust.

This is just an example of how the eyes are used to convey the attractiveness of body language.

Here are some more signs of body language through the eyes.

Pupil dilation

However, there are several possibilities for pupil dilation, z. B. in low light conditions! A good reason is when physical or emotional pleasure occurs. The pupils of the eyes get bigger and are a magnet for body language. For this reason, they are generally known as bedroom eyes and are generally attractive to someone who stares at them. This is one of the reasons why low-light environments, such as clubs, make people more attractive or attractive.

Look

You can tie a person or an object, maybe a beautiful view, a sculpture, a painting. This is so powerful that staring can make other people get trapped by your gaze and follow your eyes.

Looking at the attraction of body language

Of all the signs of nonverbal communication, ophthalmology is probably the most intriguing. It is assumed that the eyes (i.e. our visualization) are the windows of the soul". I agree with you because your eyes reveal your inner thoughts and feelings.

Even more surprising is the fact that you can use eye-body language to build trust and make people love you. Here is how:

Eye contact is the key.

In approximately 70% of cases, you need to make eye contact if you want to express your sincerity and respect. The unconscious avoidance of eye contact gives the impression of dishonesty, shyness, fear, or humiliation.

If you constantly avoid eye contact, you may be perceived as insecure, unreliable, or even fraudulent. Although this may not be the case, this is the normal impression that people have of someone who cannot look him straight in the eye.

If you are too shy or fear eye contact, just look at the bridge of the nose, or the part between the eyes and they will think you are looking at them.

Pay attention to your eye-body language.

Some people unconsciously send body language signals that offend others. So be sensitive to your eye movements. Do not roll your eyes, as this indicates irritation.

Their eyes light up when they are in a comfortable or happy state, and they look bored when they are alone or depressed. Therefore, if you have problems or are in a bad mood, it may be a good idea to reorganize your appointment with an important person. Your eyes unconsciously send signals for your mood or mental state.

Show your eyes

Avoid wearing sunglasses because covering your eyes can give the impression of hiding something. Because the eyes are very expressive, it means that people should not know how you feel or think that they should not see your eyes. In addition, the other party feels uncomfortable because he does not know if he is looking at her or not.

Know what the body language of the eye of human's means.

How do you know if people are paying attention to you? They will know when they make eye contact while nodding, smiling or leaning closer.

If they raise their eyebrows, they may want to say or clarify something, end the conversation or disagree with something you said.

People who deliberately avoid your eyes and do not intend to look at you may not be interested in talking to you. However, you may decide to stay away from them.

Don't look if you don't like to be seen.

Be aware of people who may be offended when you look at them. Some people avoid eye contact due to extreme shyness. So don't contribute to their discomfort by looking at them.

Some cultures may consider eye contact as a negative or irreverent act. So be sensitive when you meet people from different cultures and adapt to their convictions.

In addition to reading body language, you should also check other nonverbal cues to get a better idea of what they think or feel.

CHAPTER 6

UNDERSTANDING THE PSYCHOLOGY OF BODY LANGUAGE

It is well known that body language has a significant impact on interpersonal relationships. Even simple hand movements can be interpreted in different ways. To complicate matters further, other body movements and facial expressions can alter the meaning of a hand gesture. Therefore, it may not be as easy as body language seems to read.

People often don't notice it, but their body movements are an example of involuntary behavior that can convey their thoughts to others. Because different personality types have different behaviors, you should be aware of how you are moving, since people can often measure it based on the behaviors you indicate.

It is essential to remember that the gestures we call body language not only say a lot about other people but that these physical expressions of what we think can also say more about ourselves. Body language can be described as a mirror of the soul since what we really feel is usually reflected in our posture and body movements.

The way we behave can tell others what emotions we experience.

The interesting thing about nonverbal communication is that it is a product of our biology, environment, and culture. Perhaps that is why body language can point others to our attitudes. We can inherit certain properties that influence how we project ourselves in others, but we tend to use different forms of nonverbal communication depending on our relationship with others. For example, your work colleagues are probably presented differently to your family members. Perhaps because the comfort zone varies, in certain situations it becomes more careful, which affects the way it reacts.

Without a doubt, the power lies in the way you physically present yourself to others. While some gestures are intentional, many reactions of the body when we communicate with others seem more involuntary. Unfortunately, unconscious body language sometimes makes us reveal things that we don't want others to know about us. There are a few numbers of physical signs that can give other clues about our emotional state or what we feel.

If we realize it or not, we observe and process the body language of others, especially when we speak. Facial expressions and hand gestures make the conversation more meaningful. If we were not aware of these things, someone else's words probably would not have the same effect.

One way to interpret the signals of others more accurately is to be more self-aware. Pay attention to your gestures and movements when you speak. Try to understand the connection between your nonverbal communication and the words that express a thought. By learning to read your own body language, you can begin to understand the interactions you have with others.

Children are an excellent example of how our innate body language works. Especially young children often communicate their feelings non-verbally, even if they begin to develop vocabulary. A child's actions can usually tell him if he is angry or unhappy. Young children and preschoolers seem to have a natural ability to express themselves physically. Similarly, babies and young children can read our body language very well.

Interestingly, the gestures that children develop to communicate their needs can help their brains develop and then contribute to verbal communication. From the beginning, babies pay close attention to an adult's face and focus on the eyes while talking to them. How do you know that? Genetics is the most logical reason; maybe the eyes are the windows of the soul!

Communication is an essential aspect of the human being. We not only interact with the words we speak and the actions we perform but also with the way we use our bodies in relation to our environment and others. Unpublished communication is often the most effective because sometimes words don't express everything we want to say and say so much about us that we don't notice anything if we don't realize it.

We often do not realize what our body expresses, but body language is an effective means of communication to take into account. It points to more subtle signs that point to it

Sometimes you can say something with words, but your body language can say something completely different. For example, when you try to find friends and show someone that you are friendly, but in a defensive and aggressive attitude, your message seems confusing and confusing. It is essential to be aware of this so that you can better communicate with the body, what you want to convey to others. It gives your words more depth and power if you can support them with conscious body language.

To know more about your body language, stop, and pay attention to what you are doing. It takes practice to learn to master the habits and peculiarities it may have. The ability to learn more safely is worth not only in personal relationships but also in a professional environment. If you know the message you are transmitting and are using it to project the image you want, you will get much more advantage during a job interview. You will also avoid projecting an image that you may not want to project, such as insecurity, even if your words are safe. Your body language will express a different story and undermine what you are trying to communicate.

As you learn to protect the body language you want, you become a better communicator and interact at a deeper level with others. It is important to know that part of body language has different meanings for people from different cultures, but there are some universal similarities. Consider what you transmit in each situation and how to control your actions. That way, you can avoid most of the pitfalls in your path. It also alerts you to the body language that others use to get more information about the interactions.

Knowledge of body language is a very important skill. With practice and self-knowledge, you can connect with others and understand more than the words that other people speak.

You will definitely notice a completely new reaction from people as you release the strength of body language. We all communicate nonverbally, even without having to think about it.

If you want to have a strong advantage in life, you must convey the correct signs of body language, with or without saying anything else. Here we explain how to use the power of body language.

The procedure

First, you must establish a territory to harness the power of body language. You are responsible and trust everything you do or will say during the expected interview.

Separate the feet without completely blocking the knees. Allow your shoulders rest, keep your hands at your sides (never in your pockets) and breathe gently. Take an open posture and enjoy a warm and welcoming facial expression as if you were willing to communicate. Depending on the situation, you can smile.

Using the power of body language while conversing

Face the other person or your audience directly and make as much eye contact as possible throughout the conversation. The assent, raises your eyebrows, and brings your head close, shows that you are listening.

Do not cross your arms, do not look at the floor and do not put your hands in your pockets. These may subliminally show that you are not interested.

If you have comments, you can see them negatively but respectfully, such as: For example, raising your eyebrows, pressing your lips and raising your palm forward, as if telling the person to pause.

Key to trust

Much of your body language can show how safe, interested, bored, annoying, or nervous you are. Keep your head in the conversation to show that you are very involved in the conversation.

You can also use some hand movements to highlight a point. When you list things, it is better to use each of your fingers while mentioning each point to help your audience keep track.

Tempo helps you create more ground if you want to communicate with a larger amount. It also shows confidence in your part when thinking about more things to say. Balancing arms and climbing are also good indicators of self-confidence.

Acts performed by a self-confident person say more than words. And when people say "action," they mean more than just hand movement.

The body helps send messages that are clearer than what comes out of the mouth, regardless of whether the person knows it or not.

When a person feels nervous or insecure, he shows his body language. They will not have the power of body language.

For the same reason, of course, he would also show his confidence if he is sure of himself.

CHAPTER 7

THE NEED FOR A CONFIDENT BODY LANGUAGE

Of course, between an uncertain and self-conscious body language, the latter is the most advantageous.

When a person feels safe, he also seems to have confidence. And if he does, he gives them a kind of aura that demands respect and attention from others.

Such type of trust can also be useful if someone is trying to find a job or have a customer invest in their business.

Nobody wants to hire someone, much less trust, who doesn't feel safe.

Lack of trust means a lack of skills, talents, and skills. This is something you should avoid sending others about you.

Now that it has been determined that self-confident physical gestures are much better than insecure gestures, the question arises of how exactly it does that.

Here are some practical tips to learn safe body language.

APPEARANCE AND COMFORT

No matter what a person does to appear safe, it would be impossible to look like this if he doesn't feel well at all.

The first step in looking safe is to feel safe. The least one can do to have that feeling is to make sure they are well taken care of, d. H. Showes, with clean and tidy clothes, brush your teeth, comb your hair, etc.

Looking good and feeling good is the first step in having the confidence you need.

TIGHTEN THE HANDLE

As mentioned earlier, when trying to find a job or induce a client to invest in your business, it is essential to provide safe information about body language. And one way to do it is to shake hands with firmness and sincerity.

It is wrong to doubt when shaking someone's hand.

What you should do is stretch your hand with confidence and shake others firmly.

SMILE BUT DON'T FALSE

A safe body language also shows that a person feels good.

This means that you are satisfied with the things in your environment and, therefore, it is a good source of positive energy.

Let this trust radiate from within through a real and beautiful smile.

IT DOESN'T GO FOR HIS ARMS AND HANDS

There are two things that a person should never do in his entire socializing life.

These two things cross your arms, and the other put your hands in your pocket.

The first shows arrogance, the second boredom, and indifference.

Your body language conveys a lot about what kind of person you are.

It is a sure way to convey confidence in yourself.

Start applying these practical, but simple, self-confident tips for body language, and soon you will radiate more security and confidence in all the people and situations you encounter.

Safety precautions

Avoid playing with objects such as pencils, coins, and shirt buttons. Practice feeling comfortable with your arms attached to your sides. If you intend to be cautious, you can frustrate them as necessary, but reopen with new and accepted ideas. You can sit down if it is correct or necessary but never bend over. Covering your mouth after speaking indicates a false statement or lie.

It is also not recommended to point your finger directly at your audience unless you wish to discriminate or accuse. Be very careful when you touch the other person because through real contact you will go beyond the limits of body language. Remember, in body language; it is your body that speaks for you. It's fair that you dress well enough to convey your message without undue distractions properly. The power of body language is fascinating; Use it wisely.

CHAPTER 8

BODY LANGUAGE IN UNLINED COMMUNICATION

Everyone knows the saying, "facts say more than words." This is the ancient wisdom that is universally applicable, no matter what culture, country or situation you are in. Even in places where language can be a barrier, communication is completely possible because all people speak the same universal body language. Understanding body language is important to help you understand the whole message that people convey to you. This message is deeper than the words you can use on the surface. With some basic guidelines, you can read people better and understand their body language.

Non-verbal communication

Body language can be more accurately called "nonverbal communication" or something that says something to someone without using words. This is not just a universal attitude or sign language; Body language also manifests itself in things like facial expressions, tone of voice, eye contact, and many other things. Everything that another person makes of the person receiving a message is considered body language. For example, if you ask someone a question and they respond, they quickly look the other way. This is a fairly accurate indicator that he is probably lying at least partially. However, this is not 100 percent correct. If they are extremely nervous or shy, they may have the same reaction.

The value of the ability to read people for what they do not say is to know all the common signs and indicators that most people can show, observe, and do according to their body language. You see, draw conclusions.

According to a study carried out over time, non-verbal communication when speaking represents approximately 55%, while the proportion is only 7%, while the rest is the vocal component of communication, which represents 38%. This nonverbal component of communication is called body language. In everyday life, your body language influences how you perceive it when interacting with others and, in the best case, has a positive effect. Your movements, gestures, and facial expressions are very important factors that you should carefully consider when you intend to use body language to improve your presentation.

How do you say what I would call the vocal component; (His voice and how he uses it) and what he does not say in words, what is the nonverbal component of communication; It's fine, and they are synchronized. In other words, what you say must be in line with how you say it and what you don't say. To receive a complete message, all three must be in one. If there is a separation between these elements, your message will be negatively affected. Imagine a man in love telling his eight-year-old friend that he wants to marry her while he frowns and crosses his arms. However, it is important to learn and practice how to use body language effectively to spread your message. The idea behind this is to reconcile what your body says with your words to give the outstanding presentation you have always wanted.

As a successful speaker, focus on using positive or open body language to improve the reception of your message to your audience. Common examples of positive body language are open arms, good eye contact, open chest, and wide legs, smiling faces, etc., which are proven methods to show warmth, comfort, and accessibility. I learned that people sometimes buy things that are based on emotion rather than logic. Your ability to interact emotionally with your audience can also depend largely on your body language. This is the most striking communication element, depending on who is watching and listening. Body language is more complete than this, but for a speaker to speak in front of an audience, some of the examples above may be sufficient.

You should avoid negative body language, such as an epidemic, as this can affect your message and decrease your credibility in the presence of your audience. Examples include arms crossed, frowning on the face, pointing the finger or shaking an object on the face of your audience.

Body language will always be an essential part of communication, so you should be able to control it and use it effectively to add value to your presentation.

I am sure that you have heard before that body language is often the true communication that takes place behind words. Some say they represent 70% of the communication; others go even more than 90%. In any case, it should now be clear to you that knowledge of body language can give you a vital benefit when it comes to winning your potential partner.

I.used some of these techniques, and I would like to tell you that they are really very powerful and definitely work. Paying careful attention to the nonverbal cues you show others gives you the key advantage in the game of attraction. Knowing these powerful body language secrets helps you see when someone is interested in you. The following body language tips have been compiled from the best information available on the Internet.

1. Always remember to smile often, but make sure you don't feel obligated or wrong when people take it and assume something is wrong. The smile calms the other person and shows self-confidence, a positive attitude, and kindness. It shows the other person that you are primarily a socially adapted person.

2. Physically open your body to show that you are interested in the other person. This means that you look directly into their eyes and face them or sit in front of them. Don't go overboard and go straight to your face at a small angle that shows you're interested, but it's still a bit challenging and a little mysterious. Never cross your arms, move your ankles, clench your fists, or hold your drink or any object between you and your potential client. This shows that you are nervous in the situation or that you prefer to be alone on a subconscious level.

3. Maintain eye contact, but do not look at the person, unless you pretend to be a stalker. Look for a few seconds when you make a point, then

slowly look away. In fact, try to slow down all your actions, blink slowly, speak calmly, walk slowly and safely. This shows that you are not nervous or rushed, but a calm and cold person who has everything under control.

4. In your posture, try to keep your feet about shoulder-width apart, and be firmly rooted in the ground as if it were part of the ground and the ground itself. Don't be like a statue at the same time. Move from time to time a little, but do not mix with your feet all the time or play with your hands. Do not to put your hands in your pocket, especially not in your pocket. Put your thumbs in jeans pockets. It is better to keep the arms and hands at the sides, slightly bent and relaxed at the elbow.

5. Keep your head up and chest out, but do not overdo it because there is a very fine line between self-confidence and snobbery. Breathe slowly and deeply through your stomach, not your chest. Never exhale as if you were stressed.

6. When speaking, calmly and confidently use many hand movements. Express yourself through different shades, facial expressions, and gestures. There is a very fine line here. Then do nothing radical. If you have a monotonous voice, you must work to improve it and trust me. I used to have the most monotonous voice, and it can be

changed. Try singing out loud in your car or in the shower, keep talking to people and try to be more expressive. Repetition is the key here.

That should keep you busy always. Remember to continue working until it becomes second nature. First, you can return to old habits, but remember to make a mental note when you do this and try to change immediately. Eventually, all these things will infiltrate, and you will have created a new habit, a more assertive, quieter, sexier, and more attractive version of you!

Next, I want to examine some of the body language cues that women emit when they find a man attractive and are interested in knowing him better. Often, women send very obvious and not so obvious evidence of body language. If you know the following secrets of female body language, you have a clear advantage over the competition.

- If you see a woman from afar and suddenly she has eye contact and then looks down, she is most likely interested. If she looks at you and then looks left or right, she probably won't be so in love with you. So don't waste your time with her.

- One of the most obvious signs that she is attracted to you is a broad, bright smile and bright eyes as if she were looking at a cute baby. You can also easily lick your lips or show your tongue by licking the front of your teeth. Sometimes it can be very subtle, she is not aware of her actions, but it is you.

- Everything is in the eyes, as they say, if she continues to look deeply into your eyes and can't help it, then she is definitely interested. Look back into her eyes and see if her pupils are dilated when she does. If It is so; then she sees something she wants, then you can even bother her a little and tell her that her pupils are dilated. I am sure that will surprise her quite a bit. Other things to consider are raised eyebrows, or if she winks at you from a distance, she can also shake her eyelashes and blink more than normal.

- There are many different things a woman will do with her body to point out that interest in these things is one of the most common.

He often stands up to show certain parts of his body that he finds sexy, with the breasts protruding, the spine curved and the head bowed.

Usually, he stands in a ¾ or lateral posture to emphasize the curvature of his body.

* Often plays without realizing it. The most common places are the neck, legs, chest, and throat. Pay attention because this is a clear indication that you want to be approached.

* A woman will want to show you her best looks, she will adjust her clothes and hair, this includes straightening her dress, fixing her hair and jewelry. Do not be surprised if she often disappears into the bathroom. Usually, she checks her appearance to look her best.

Knowing even these basic body language cues can be a great benefit when it comes to attracting your potential partner. Remember to be aw

Nonverbal communication is the message that our body language transmits between people, such as: as facial expressions, head movements, posture and actions, clothing, mannerism, personality behavior, etc.

You have probably heard that 55% of the total impact of our communication depends on our body language (nonverbal communication). The tone of our voice determines another 38%. And only 7% is determined by verbal communication.

Researchers have discovered that some specific actions in our body language have certain meanings.

Let us examine this illustration, the movements and gestures of the head and face provide information about the nature of the emotions that are expressed. Posture and tension reveal the intensity of the feeling.

A body language that I find very noticeable in people is the facial grimace when they listen to someone who is trying to express or explain something.

This is quite rude, and it's like saying, "Come on, can't you say it fluently?", "Why do you find it difficult to talk?" Instead of waiting patiently and listening to the person as good as he/she can.

Another type of body language example is for someone to nod during the presentation of a seminar. This says something about the feelings of the participant towards the seminar, the speaker or the company: the moderator is bored, or the participant is completely disinterested and disrespectful.

Be careful with all these analyze of body language. Too many people read a book or learn a body language course and begin to exaggerate the scrutiny of others.

The fact that a book says "cross your arms over your chest" is a sign of domination, or lack of cooperation does not mean that anyone who adopts that attitude expresses that message. Absolutely

How many times have you done and not cooperated? Often, this attitude is simply because you are tired of hanging your arms at your sides during a long and long speech! It is a comfortable position. I often do it without any negative meaning.

I have seen some of the most positive people at the meetings, listening attentively to a presenter, being the most cooperative and waiting for what the presenter said or did, all with arms crossed over their chest!

Another common theme of body language is that the speaker's eyes move during speech temporarily in space. This must mean several things. I even saw the listeners staring at the ceiling because the speaker's eyes focused on him for a moment.

Some studies have even found that the line of sight even indicates what information is "recovered" in the brain (i.e., left eye, right brain, right eye, left brain), etc.

I saw people looking in the corner of a room while talking just because there was a distraction there!

The mechanism for the right and left brain has a lot of truth to offer, but sometimes "experts" get carried away too much. No one understands anything about the brain yet.

Most people simply "seek" their thoughts. If you look closely, you will find that people occasionally interrupt eye contact while talking, but constantly concentrate while listening. Most of us do that.

Separating eye contact with the listener does not necessarily mean that the individual hides something from his listener, or that he is lying, as an "expert" will tell you. Sometimes they can do that, but more often they don't. These conclusions are results of studies of behavioral extremes.

Instead of saying that the movement or separation of the eyes in one way or another when talking to another is a hoax, teachers should say: "... it could mean cheating or lying, but it usually means that person looks for words shy or uncomfortable in the presence of authority or a stranger, or simply not aware of a bad habit.

And there may be a complete list of other reasons. Shyness is often the cause of such behavior. My sweet seventy-five-year-old mother is so shy that she can't even look at the supermarket cashier in the eye!

Maybe someone has never been taught to communicate. In fact, this habit is eliminated after a person has noticed and worked to correct it; in other words, after having exceeded himself conscientiously.

Politicians or public relations people learn communication and body language as part of their experience or education. I see it all the time, and it seems amazing how some of your views can also be constantly set on the phone while talking. Some are born or raised for that; it is part of their personality type.

But someone who does not work in a public environment was not informed about it, is not as experienced and may have never heard of it! Make your goal to observe this and then start training. It is not easy, or you discover that you are well. Then appreciate this fact and feel good.

People communicate much more than words. In fact, more than sixty percent of the communication is not spoken at all but is shown to everyone in their body language. More importantly, body language always tells the truth, although sometimes the words people use can be lies. If you want to really understand what people communicate, you need to listen with your eyes to what their bodies say.

Thousands of books on body language have been written. They try to explain the meaning of each physical movement: move away, sit down, lean forward, bend your arms, and even scratch your nose. Well, the theories are good and good. But if we want to understand what the body requires of us, we need a better tool than a list of body movements and what they mean.

The best tool to decode body language is a technique that simply encodes a person's body language in green, yellow, or red.

Green Body Language indicates that your audience is open to your words and ideas. Whenever you see a green body language, you will know that your words are considered carefully. And then you keep talking. Green body language includes strong eye contact, nod, bow, open hands, smile, and the listener's gaze on the speaker.

Yellow body language indicates that your listeners have something in their head. You may want to make a point. You may have misunderstood its meaning, and now you want to clarify it. You may be bored and want to end your conversation. Or you accidentally pressed and bothered an emotional hot button. For some reason, they are not satisfied with what you say and, unless you deal with what causes the yellow signal, they will not communicate. Yellow body language includes, but is not limited to, hitting with your finger, closing a hand, frowning, making faces, raising an eyebrow, raising a finger, breathing suddenly, leaning back, bowing your head, crossing your arms and walk away or not look at a speaker.

Red body language means that your listeners do not listen and do not want to listen. They are angry and upset or nervous and intimidated. Red body language shows that you are in danger of causing a misunderstanding as your point of view continues. Therefore, it is better to fix the relationship before continuing. If people turn their backs on you and keep talking, you ignore a very strong signal and make the situation even worse. Red body language includes, among others, forming a fist, moving away, shaking your head, invading personal space, refusing eye contact, shaking hands, frozen postures and any sudden or violent movement.

Now I bet you know at least one car driver who behaves as if the colors of a traffic light had the following meaning: red, stop; Go green; Yellow, go faster.

Have you ever rushed for a yellow traffic light to beat red? More importantly, have you ever broken someone's yellow body language to express your opinion?

When people see a yellow body language, they generally push their logic instead of slowing down and making their listeners catch up. They ignore even the most obvious bodily cues, find disagreements, find misunderstandings, and wonder why nobody listens to them.

Brian Tracy, the author of Advanced Selling Strategies, suggests that the difference between socially intelligent and socially incompetent people is often determined by the person's ability to read and respond effectively to body language. Most people read body language very well. However, few are able to respond quickly and effectively to the communication of this body language.

We tend to push our words when the signals coming from people silently shout for us to give in. Someone walks away from us, but we follow this person out of the room. Someone raises a hand in our direction, but we raise our voices and begin to steam.

If we do not respond intelligently to bodily signals, there are communication problems everywhere. If someone sends you green body signals, it means they are in touch and communicates. Therefore, you should feel free to keep talking.

However, if someone sends you yellow signals from the body, you should slow down and develop understanding instead of continuing to talk. Every time you run through a yellow signal, you run the risk of colliding with a belief, entering an opinion, or hitting an ego. So slow down and put green signs. You can always clarify your point of view later when the person you are communicating with is open again and focused on what you have to say. If you wait for a green signal before continuing, you are more likely to notice the person you are talking to

She will really listen.

The red signs of the body indicate that the relationship has collided. You better stop everything and retire. Give them the space needed to maneuver, otherwise they both sink. Give them some margin until they cool and send green signals again.

CHAPTER 9

POSITIVE THINKING AND BODY LANGUAGE

Body language is something we often don't realize, but sometimes it can say more than our words could say. That's why it is so important to pay attention to the language of your body and always be aware of what others say.

Body language is the movement of your body, the way you hold it, and facial expressions, including eye movements. It often reflects our attitude and sometimes contradicts what our words say.

When our bodies and words do not match, people probably believe in how their body reacts, because it is often something unconscious that reveals the truth.

When you try to implement positive thinking in your life, you must also implement positive body language. If you are really committed to a positive mindset, your body will follow. However, if you don't feel positive with your whole heart, your body movements can betray you.

It is very important that you realize how your body reacts if you want to incorporate positive thinking into your life. Actually, you may want to learn about the body and the way it reveals things, so you can see how you should not react and not let your positive thinking and attitude affect you.

A good example is a smile. You have probably smiled at a stranger before.

What happened It probably happened that they smiled back. Do you know that the smile has probably made you smile at someone and so on, while your smile becomes contagious?

The smile can affect people. A smile you give to a stranger may be the motivation that someone needs to be happy that day, instead of being moody. You never know

A smile not only says that you are contagious, but that you are also happy. It means you have a good day and want to share it with them. A smile is a powerful body language.

It's also common for you to have a positive experience when you approach a situation happily with a positive body movement. People are more likely to help you and do everything possible to make sure you get what you need if you do it in a positive way.

You should definitely learn about body language and avoid negative body language. At first, it will take a little effort to train so that your body does not use negative body language. Body language can tell a dead person that their true feelings are not positive. Therefore, positive thinking also includes positive body language.

Body language says a lot about how we think and what we demonstrate with our body behavior. Our body can tell another person that we feel defeated, tired, or competent. This language is often inadvertently used to manipulate others and avoid unwanted results. The internal dialogue used to map a result can determine what behavior we will have during a real event.

A positive perspective of what we want, with the expectation of success, will help us achieve an intention and realize it. On the other hand, thinking too much about what we want to avoid can make us fail. The thoughts we have taken into account a possible confrontation can put our bodies in a position of defeat. Our body can reveal to another how we expect it to respond. People constantly fulfill our wishes. Apathy can remain in our body language until our image-stimulating thoughts have changed.

We often get exactly what we want to avoid, with the use of our body language and the thoughts behind it. We play a game of the show, and we have our bodies and send a strong message to the people. We can say one while our body sends a very different message. Normally our body language determines the result. We influence other people. The way someone else reacts to us depends on what we reveal with the use of our body.

Most people are passive-aggressive, and their internal thoughts and dialogues are to blame. For a statement to be effective, a person must have authority in their body language that corresponds to their words. Powerful gestures, along with strong words and speech sounds, are a defense. In addition, it is only a sign that the person has managed to think negatively about an outcome and become doubtful.

Moreover, a confident-sounding voice, backed by uncertain thinking, cannot disguise what the body reveals.

Thinking with a positive attitude and eliminating negative inner dialogues can create a behavior that helps us. We can choose to incorporate fears and doubts into our body language. We can create an appearance of self-confidence and self-esteem if we so wish. Expectations that are built up in our heads determine, among other things, our body language. Think positively and the body will follow!

CHAPTER 10

NEGATIVE BODY LANGUAGE

Her body language speaks volumes about you as a man. It is the most important factor, whether you can arouse the interest of an attractive woman or you are completely bumped. I've already written about how you can dress women with your body language. Now I will explore how a negative body language can affect your dating / social life. It shows some body language traits that may prevent you from taking in women. Imagine that all these scenarios are a nightclub.

You see a girl dressing you. She is sitting alone at a table. You get up and walk toward them with long strides, holding your head as if you are looking down on people. You come to her table and stand there looking down on her. First, long steps indicate that you are in a hurry, and women do not see it as self-control. There is a difference between walking with your head held high and walking so high that you look down on people. One shows self-confidence and self-esteem, and the other shows a man who seems to think he is somehow better than everyone else. Women see this as narcissistic and do not want to have anything to do with selfish men. Reaching over and possibly frightening an unsuspecting woman is one of the worst things to do. They show the woman that you are a tyrant and that you see her as an object by not sitting down and equaling her, let alone frightening her in the process. When you see a woman you want to address, everything begins and ends with your body language. Starting from the moment you get up from your place to the moment you reach it, all the women are watching and judging you, including those you care about. If your body language is negative, you will not get good results and rejection is guaranteed.

Are you one of the shy men who sit alone and watch every woman entering the club? If you see a woman who interests you, you have no idea how to approach her. Instead of facing the agony of approaching, are you trying to convey your message by staring at it? To stare at a woman is not a good thing. It makes her uncomfortable, just as it makes us uncomfortable when someone stares at us. It provokes a "fight or flight" reaction in a woman. If you think so, how do you react when you stare directly into the eyes of a strange dog? The dog gets pretty annoying, starts barking and when chained, he'll probably try to break it to get at you. A stare is a form of aggression. If you are staring at a woman, she sees you as aggressive, and if you have the courage to approach, the "fight" will be a bad rejection, and the "escape" will be you leaving the club because you just managed to stay uncomfortable for her. Instead of using stare as a technique to interest a woman, go home and work on yourself so you lose the shyness and learn to be self-confident so that you can approach an attractive woman instead of you next time to starve and expel before you come to your table to sell yourself.

The following is something I have heard from all women in my own social environment, and it is the number 1 behavior that not only rejects women but can even eliminate them from a club. Women refer to this as "club harassment." I saw it myself and saw the impact it has on every woman in the club. I will give you the scenario that I have used as an example to show the strongly negative and frightening form of body language that it is. I was in a club with some friends a few weeks ago, and I noticed that this guy was standing next to one of my girlfriends and calling her Names. He looked at her very carefully. She also noticed and thought he was one of those shy guys who didn't have the guts to get close. He stood up to use the restroom, and I noticed that the guy had disappeared. When I returned to the table, she was very upset. This boy not only followed her and stood near the women's bathroom, but also followed her outside, watching her silently as she leaned against a wall when she smoked a cigarette. At that moment of his tirade, I looked to my right and saw the same guy leaning against a wall about fifty feet away, looking at Samantha again. I looked around the club and noticed that some other women were looking in his direction, probably because he also followed them. Samantha was furious with this guy because her body language and actions were so cowardly that she actually felt attacked by him. He had aroused his hatred without saying a word. Samantha told me that women sometimes meet this type of guy in a club and their response is: "Please, don't call me." He also said that some women would get the gorilla to accompany them to their vehicles or wait for their taxis with them. Women are afraid of these men, as they should be. Your body language reeks of hostility. That particular night, I actually found myself in a combat or flight mode. If I am in this mode as a man, how do you think that affects women? It is a terrible technique to find a wife. In the best case, you get a "bad" dance with one because they are too scared to say no. In the worst case you will be expelled.

A negative body language is the strongest antipathy towards women. This must be resolved immediately if you ever want to reach the approach phase. Women do not give men who seem intimidating the time of day when they rise above them, and they almost dare to reject a woman. Their thoughts about bullying are that they probably talk a lot with their hands with their wives, so rejection is a certainty. Covering or bandaging women is objectifying women. They are not objects. They are human. You won't wear a woman who does that. For anyone who thinks it is a challenge for women to chase women in clubs to show their attraction, they quickly lose that attitude.

No one likes to be persecuted. It causes a combat or flight condition in both cases. It is the number one fork and will probably take you out of the club or fight with someone because a woman who feels threatened will try to seize a completely different type just to stay away from you. Most men protect women and want to treat them on a personal level. All these negative features of body language are a serious barrier to access women. These qualities have to disappear, and more positive body language should simply replace them before even thinking about approaching a woman. However, not everything is always lost. It only takes practice and an internal look to see what kind of man you are and what kind of man you want to be. The rest will follow, of course.

Aggressive body language, whether passive or combative, is never comfortable when you are close, especially if you are the person receiving. And although some people are better at dealing with fear and frustration than others, we have all participated at some point in our lives or are aggressive in nature.

As a human being, anger is a normal and to some extent, healthy human emotion when expressed in moderation. However, when a seemingly small nuisance explodes in much greater anger, we will not only test how to control it but also how to handle it when someone you know well uses it to intimidate you.

First, it is important to realize that aggressive body language does not need to involve physical contact, but may include other methods of intimidation that are equally threatening and inappropriate. Examples of aggressive body language can be:

- Complicated facial expressions such as frowning, pointed lips, teasing, and grunting. The intense eyes that look at you cause deep intimidation.

- Intimidation when entering, touching, pushing, or unnecessarily pushing a person's personal area.

– Use insulting or threatening gestures, dare to attack or make sudden movements to catch the enemy without preparation.

It is not necessary to study body language psychology to know that aggressive body language is unacceptable to most people, and although it seems to come from a position of strength, such behavior is, in fact, a clear indication that the person is not the inner strength, the ability to communicate or the ability of people to deal adequately with their anger problems and personal problems. If you know someone who is, or if you know you are fighting aggression, you must first realize that it is a problem, then you can do something about it.

Finding yourself in a circumstance where someone expresses aggressive body language, in such a state of anger, one of the best ways to deal with it is to communicate with your body language. If the person in question is so involved in your aggression, using sensible and calm words may be helpful, but it may not be enough to cool the situation.

Instead, try to remain calm, but don't be shy about what is happening. Allow them know that you are not afraid, get up, and stand on your floor. If you stay strong using non-aggressive body language, you can dispel the situation and continue as the best person.

If you are the person who has difficulty controlling your aggression, it is important first to recognize the problem. During an altercation, try to get out of the situation and take a break, seek the advice of a neutral friend or seek the help of a counselor or a person with whom you feel comfortable.

Aggressive body language can make you feel in control, but in the end, using those tactics can make you and your fellow men feel even more distressed and dissatisfied.

Body language is a part of communication that very few learn. However, it constitutes the bulk of what we use for communication and is generally much more accurate than the words we use. I will give you some reasons why body language is so important, and then I will give you a brief questionnaire to see how well you understand the meaning.

They say that actions speak louder than words, and sometimes we can communicate things without the help of a single word. We can shrug and say without saying a word: "I don't know." We can raise your eyebrows and say, "I'm sorry, did I hear you well?" We can turn our hands and say, "I don't know what else to say, that's all I have." And we can point our noses to indicate that the other person "has done well."

Some of the things we say with our bodies can help us confirm the reason we say it. Simply saying "I don't know" has nothing to do with adding the following gestures. We can raise our hands while raising our eyebrows and turning our smiles as we slightly lower the lower lip and look to the side. Now we have also made someone laugh and perhaps the pressure of ourselves or the other person, who was a little nervous, not knowing what we did not know.

In addition, it can help us observe a person's body language if someone does not tell us the truth and nothing but the truth. I will be showing you some signs that someone is lying. Often, a person who does not tell the truth or the whole truth does not want to make eye contact because he fears that the eyes are the windows of their lying souls. However, there are also other signs of lies. A person who does not tell the whole truth can clear his throat, stutter or change his tone as if trying to divert his attention from his lie or stop him, so he has time to find a valid or plausible answer. In addition, tapping or humming, blushing, placing your hand on your face, avoiding or raising your shoulders can be signs that you are uncomfortable talking because you are not revealing the truth.

Other important function of body language is to express our feelings for what we are talking about. Body language can assist us determine how someone feels about what they say. For example, a person may tell his boss that he would like to accept that, but his body language may indicate that he is not happy with that. This can be an important deal with which a manager can determine who is the best person for the job. If your heart is not there, you can do a proper job if another employee turns that little job into a customer for life.

Body language can be the deciding factor in a job interview. If the candidate's body language conveys that he is familiar with the subject and that he is confident, he will be more likely to get a job, especially in this difficult labor market. We have already said that part of body language is interpreted as unpleasant and uncontrolled. These are some of the same characteristics that make an applicant less safe and comfortable.

In a friendship, body language may indicate that someone is paying attention or does not really care what the other person is saying. If you rely on the conversation, this is an indication that this person is interested in hearing what the other person is saying. Leaning back would mean that he was selfless or that he felt superior. If you lean forward and are close to speaking, you may indicate that someone is trying to convince the other person or dominate the conversation aggressively. Listening to someone without having eye contact means that you are not really paying attention, but are waiting for your opportunity to speak. This gives your friend the feeling that he doesn't really care about him and his comments, and that he may not be listening carefully when it is his turn to speak in a conversation.

A lot of people mistakenly accept that they can only succeed if they are effective speakers and use motivational and persuasive rhetoric. Being a good speaker is, in most cases, certainly a positive capital, but mere rhetoric alone rarely convinces most people. Most people are judged by their body language than by the content of their words, and this body language is always the result of a combination of professional training and self-confidence.

Body language has many factors. These include eye contact, posture, how and where to place the arms and hands, eye movements and eye contact, gestures, etc. Do you sleep when you are with other people or are you standing? If you don't stay, is your "good" posture rigid and upright or relaxed and cozy? Are your arms and hands relaxed or your arms, for example, rigid in front of you? What about your eyes? Are you directly with the people you are talking to, or are you looking the other way, aside, etc.? How was your facial expression? Is it solid and repellent, relaxes or smiles all the time? Which one would you feel most comfortable with? Are you constantly gesturing and turning with your arms? Do you point directly to others where your finger could make someone feel that it is almost like a weapon? Check the mirror and see what you do when you talk to others. Would you consider your body language to be supportive, comforting and positive, or would you stay away from it? It is important to think about the aura of mysticism that you transmit to others.

Your body language is often your visible part of your presentation. Speakers in large forums use PowerPoint presentations or other visual aids to reduce their attention alone. Therefore, when you are in a situation where you are in a less formal environment or where there are no visual aids available, much of the effectiveness of your presentation depends on the feeling others have of your body language. Is your body language positive or negative? Does it convey the same message as your words?

Do you get the feeling when you look at your body language, that you are friendly or seem detached? Does your body language convey a message of integrity, or is it unreliable? Body language must be your ally and not your enemy. One can better understand body language by watching the television and radio tapes of the 1960 debates by Nixon Kennedy. Most experts believe that Nixon won the debate only by listening to the radio (in other words, only the words and even how they sounded). However, the same experts believe that Kennedy was the overwhelming winner for those who watched television because of the appearance of both men, different postures, eye contact, facial expression, etc. Without a doubt, body language is something very convincing. We should spend more time understanding, improving, and focusing on aligning our body language with the message we want to convey.

If you have difficulty winning people as friends and lovers, one of the reasons may be that you have a negative body language that sends a signal that you do not want anyone to approach you. You may not be aware of your body language, but you are sending these signals to others all the time.

Even if you go to a party with the most provocative and dazzling outfit, they will probably leave you alone and ignored when you stand or sit with your arms crossed and a nervous smile on your face.

When other people see you at a party or other social situation, they will immediately evaluate you to get an idea of what type of person you are. One of the most important ways in which people perceive their personality is through their body language. If your body language sends negative signals, it will reject others.

Our body language sends signals all the time whether we say a word or not. People try to decipher the signals of our body language because they try to recognize the signals that indicate whether we are accessible or not.

If a person looks nervous, he may have restless gestures, and his eyes flutter around the room as if they were in panic. Such a person give the impression that other people are afraid and could flee quickly when someone tries to start a conversation with them.

A person who lazily falls on a sofa seems to be too relaxed. They may seem lazy who drank too much. A person who keeps all the muscles of the face and body very rigid will seem not to let anyone pass their defenses. With all these types of postures, people probably don't bother talking to you, especially if they don't know you.

Regardless of whether these are the signals you want to send with your body language, it is very likely that other people you see interpret their postures and movements in this way.

So what is a good posture if you want others to approach you? A person who is partially relaxed and partially attentive has the best chance of winning over others. Changing your negative body language to a more open attitude with relaxed gestures is a great way to start beating other people for yourself.

CHAPTER 11

BENEFIT THE BODY LANGUAGE OF THE ARMS FOR EFFECTIVE COMMUNICATION

Body language is a type of human communication that everyone uses, whether they notice it or not. Body language is also used in the business world relations; in general talks and more. We use body language in every interaction we have, no matter how little body language is used. Those who use sign language to communicate with the deaf may well understand the communicative power of body language, especially when communicating with someone unfamiliar with sign language. Body positioning, head movements, hand signals, eye contact, lip movements, and leg movements are used to send messages to those with whom we communicate. When we understand how we use and develop these communication methods, we can guide conversations and interactions in specific directions.

Take, for instance, Job interviews can be nerve-wracking, but nervousness is not necessarily a good message to the employer, as it may indicate a lack of trust or insecurity. As a body language, nervousness can be felt and make the interviewer ask more questions than you might want.

The best body language for a job interview is to calmly enter the interview room and slowly sit down on the chair. Sit straight in the chair, making sure your feet are flat on the floor. While you're talking to the Interviewer, you're just thinking of your attitude. Always use hand gestures simultaneously with your verbal conversation while the interview continues. However, you always want to make those gestures within the bounds of your verbal language. They want to demonstrate professionalism and body language can communicate this very effectively.

Eye contact as body language is a very important communication strategy. By maintaining eye contact with the person you are communicating with, the others learn that you are interested in having to say it. If you let your eyes go too far, it will indicate to others that you are bored and are not interested in having to say it. This can be harmful to you, especially if you are looking down to the ground. Eye contact is not just an interview strategy; it's just about every conversation you make.

However, there is a certain balance that must be applied to eye contact. You do not want to look like you're staring. For most people, especially women, staring is disrespectful and tends to make the other person nervous about your intentions. For example, if you're in a club or party and staring at other people, it can lead to adverse situations for you.

Facial expressions are another body language that can trigger or interrupt an interaction. A gradual, almost undetectable nod points to another person that you understand, era says it. However, if your nod is rather jerky, it may indicate that you are impatient with the other or that you cannot wait to answer. This latter display could send signals related to control issues that indicate impatience.

If you slightly tilt the nod with a gentle smile, you will receive the message that you are reachable. People like people who are approachable. However, the smile should be sincere to get the best results. A constant smile or grin in many situations may indicate that you are superficial and disingenuous. This could make you aloof.

An appropriate discussion question, along with the right body language, engages the other person more deeply in the conversation. The right body language can be the message of your stands out and dies again, and dies interest gives you the opportunity to lead the conversation.

We use our arms instinctively for both attack and defense. Our arms are a big part of our physical strength. It is no exaggeration to call our weapons. After all, we've learned to use our weapons in combat, from hitting, choking, to hitting. The natural result of this is that the body language of weapons has become an expressive mediator of aggression, domination, and strength as well as subjugation, weakness, and protection. In addition, the body language of the arm is one of the most readable areas of human body language, as it is always easy to spot as a person

The basics

Let's take a look at the basic body language of the arms before discussing a powerful tool for using the arms in communication.

Relaxed arms: the most relaxed position in which the arms can be with the hands out of the pockets at the sides. This is not aggressive or submissive. This is also the best place to meet new people since it is friendly but safe and comfortable.

Aggressive arms: any flexion of the arm muscles indicates aggression or willingness to dominate. Of course, this is the case, especially for men.

Protective arms: Holding the arms in front of the body is a sign of protection. Here the person will cover the vital organs in his chest, pharynx, or lower regions.

Arrogant arms: keeping your arms behind your back so that they are invisible is generally considered arrogant and can be seen as a real hand.

Open or inviting arms: Any person who extends their arms to expose their body gives a clear invitation signal, probably to embrace it.

Using arms in communication

To use arm body language for effective communication, you need to know two things. First, reading a person's arms shows how he feels about what he is saying (although he must also consider the context). Second, if you can get a person to change the way they hold their arms, it will change the way they feel about what they say.

Let's take a closer look.

Use the emotions associated with armed gestures to help communication.

Let's say you're talking to a business colleague who is standing with his arms crossed in front of his chest. By reading the above, you now know that you feel protected. This means that you are likely to check everything you say for signs of threat (to protect yourself from these threats). However, you want him to open, relax, and listen silently to what he has to say. How are you

In the previous case, you want the person to feel the feelings associated with holding their arms by their side so that they can create a way to make the person move their arms to that position. Maybe you'll give them something to hold, or you can talk in a relaxed mood until you let go of your arms and get back to your original subject.

The point is this: the body language of the arms is directly related to the way a person feels. When a person begins to feel protected, he moves his arms in front of his body. On the contrary, if a person moves his arms in front of his body, they will feel protected by this movement.

Do you see the body language of someone's hands when you haggle? To win more negotiations, you must feel their hands calmly. Hands express a lot of hidden info in a transaction.

There is so much information about how someone makes use of their hands. People use them to show appreciation. They show their hands to show disgust in other ways (that is, sit on their hands). Do you also use your hands while you speak? The hands give an idea of the thought process that someone has. While someone is talking, your hands add or distract the message you have sent. You do the same when you also send information.

When there is a difference between a person's words and their body language, pay more attention to their body language. It will reveal one's intention more than his words. Keep the following in mind when talking to someone. Think about it while negotiating.

Hands near the body

The closer someone is to your body, the more careful your thoughts are. You will see this announcement when someone perceives perceived threats to your well-being. Your hands are in this position to protect yourself from perceived indifference.

If you see this in a trial, it may be appropriate to reassure the other negotiator. Because of what has led you to show your cautious gesture, you may need to address that problem before you can gather the comfort you want it to evoke.

Hands with interlaced fingers

If you see a negotiator in this position, he or she may show a behavior that says it is not open to your offer, proposal, or counter offer. To confirm compliance, you should ask about the meaning of your ad (for example, I have noticed that you have closed your hands and locked your fingers). This generally means that someone (use "someone" for "If you release your fingers and open your hands while saying that everything is fine, ask him to continue." First, he has changed his body language, which has led him to be more open to you and your offers, and secondly, you have given the leadership in the negotiations and, subject on what you do with it. It will give you an idea of what caused the initial announcement that you questioned, and he will see what he wants to talk about, which will make clear what is important to him.

The hands removed the palms

Pay special attention to this gesture because it indicates that the author does not want to have any part of what made him show the gesture. You can see future distinctions by pushing this gesture outward. Also consider this gesture when the other negotiator expresses his statement that he agrees with you. In this case, your body language contradicts your true feelings. Believe that more than your words.

There are other manual signals that give an idea of the process of thinking about a negotiator. We will discuss them at another time. Consider the signals mentioned above for now. In this way, you become more attentive. This will assist you to win more discussions and everything will be fine with the world.

Remember, always negotiate!

"Body language secrets to gain more negotiation" will give you an idea of how to negotiate better by reading the other negotiator's body language. Also, the book explores in depth new negotiation strategies that can deactivate your negotiator and increase your trading profit rates.

There is more than one way of communication. Body language is the ability to communicate what you think and feel through conscious and unconscious body signals. It has become a serious study for many people. Politicians, businessmen, etc. use body language experts, both personally and to assist in negotiations. Some actors will even study body language and incorporate appropriate body cues into their actions to create a more realistic character.

Body language consists of small gestures that your body leaves unconscious when exposed to different emotions or actions. Let's take seemingly small and everyday activities like shaking hands. Shaking hands is a way of greeting or thanks, but how?

When someone gives you a superior handshake, you have several options to accept the handshake or place the handshake in an equivalent position. If your boss gives you a superior handshake, it is better to accept the handshake and show a sign of respect than to try to reverse the handshake. If you, as a seller, get a superior handshake, it is more important to turn it over so that the person becomes more receptive to what he says. There are two ways to convert a superior handshake into the same handshake. The first way is to enter the upper handshake. This allows you to turn your hand as you go. Another technique is to perform a handshake with both hands that allows you to take your hand and force it into an equal position.

While executives are more likely to use a superior handshake than executives, women better decipher the subtle language that is body language. This is probably the reason why women have "intuitions" or "suspicions" about others that normally seem correct. This capacity in women is attributed to the maternal instinct of women and their ability to decipher the needs of their newborn children. The natural ability of women to decode the signals of body language makes them more mendacious. As more people improve their body language skills, they can become powerful negotiators and evaluators of others.

CHAPTER 12

BENEFITS AND CONSEQUENCES OF AN EFFICIENT LANGUAGE

What else can you achieve with efficient body language?

Have you ever wondered what information is available in your body, how important it is and who can read it? Did you know that the interest in interpreting this realm of human behavior that is overlooked is growing? What are the advantages and consequences of this trend?

An efficient body language complements efficient organizations.

One of the major priorities of the information age has been to streamline operations and increase the efficiency of the organization. With the ubiquitous use of the spreadsheet and management software, almost no business process has been reviewed and reviewed. Although it has saved a lot of time, energy and frustration by incorporating machines and computers in our lives and our work, this intense concentration in technological solutions may have blinded us to the information that our body contains and expresses. Our body language can and often does something that our communicable mouths communicate and even sabotage. But how conscious are you when it occurs?

The power and the promise of gravity.

For example, notice how efficient the average person's relationship with gravity is. Most of us take this incredible magnetism for granted. In fact, who has time to worry about the seriousness of paying bills, selling products, and meeting people? But think about how strong the gravitational force of gravity is when it comes to keeping our world together. It even keeps our moon in place. Then you can marvel at the incredible amount of energy that many of us use to resist this inevitable power. Imagine for a moment about how much better we could feel and how much more energy we would have, how much better we could express ourselves if we were aware of gravity and worked a little more in harmony with it.

Most of us pay little or no attention to the efficiency with which we align our posture with the gravitational force. Since curiosity is an inevitable part of human nature, it was only a matter of time before the focus returned to using body language more efficiently. What if this time you are here now?

Read the basics of body language.

Walk in a crowded place and watch your peers and how they use their attitude to:

- Walk or stop forward, backward or leaning to one side and work against gravity.

- Tilt your head forward or backward noticeably out of the center of gravity.

- Rock or walk as you go.

- Point your feet in a different direction from the one you are approaching.

- Don't just shake your arms to keep your balance

- Do they mix so much when they leave that their shoes begin to wear unevenly?

Each of these non-essential movements requires energy and an effort to counteract the force that gravity exerts on them. Also, keep in mind that young children use gravity more efficiently. However, as we age and become more intelligent, we increasingly ignore the gravitational attraction of gravity. Using your energy to resist gravity is completely unnecessary and crazy when we are really trying to use our energy efficiently. If we are so blind to what our body does when it comes to our attitude, what conscious or unconscious effects can this behavior have on those with whom we communicate?

The light is on, and there is no one at home.

Notice how most of us do not seem to know what our bodies do while we spend the day. Many of these movements are the result of the unconsciousness of our body language or social conditioning to ignore it. Regardless of the benefit or consequence, it does something often enough and will create a pattern of behavior. Once a pattern exists, it does not take long to become part of your identity. For most of us, this pattern is incorporated into what they believe they are. Even with an injury, when the initial pain you want to avoid disappears, muscle pattern and tension are often forgotten and persist. Many go even further, wasting even more energy and time, complaining about how tired they feel. Does this sound like an efficient use of our resources?

Efficient body language is often unwanted information

Now you can try to inform someone about your observations. If you really dare to take on this challenge, you will be surprised at the answers you get. Most will politely apologize and will often blame an old injury. Others will be offended that you approach this as "as they are." Write down exactly how many would like to thank your advice and correct these inefficiencies immediately. When knowledge is power, you also feel the opportunity to learn something that most others ignore.

Think of a conscious and efficient body language

The most important thing is that you think about what body language, behavior patterns, and people's reactions to your comments will inform you about the people involved.

- Do these patterns make them seem more or less attractive?

- Would you be more or less inclined to hire them?

- Are you more or less interested in their advice?

- Do your age and intelligence affect how they react to you?

- Would you like someone in your family to show these patterns?

Or date someone who does that?

As an added benefit, ask yourself what your answer says about your ability to be curious, adaptable, and accessible.

What about your own body language cues?

So far, we have talked about all the other people around him. Here is your invitation to stand in front of a mirror, make a reflective inventory of all the above questions, and see how they relate to you and your body language. What does your body language say? How fast can you confirm and adjust it? By the way, how many of you know how to read it?

The gain in the understanding of conscious body language

Here, a gold mine awaits those who understand how to read, feel, and interpret what the body language of another demonstrates. There is also a jackpot for those who know what their own body language says. There is a third jackpot for those who understand that adjustment will not only make them feel healthier and happier, but it will also make them more attractive and influential. Could your body language have something to do with your success?

Body language is an influential tool that can influence the way we think and what choices we make. With a skillful application, it is possible to influence others and make them think and react strategically projecting their own body movements, facial expressions, and gestures.

Projecting powerful clues and avoiding some simple traps will help you in two simple ways:

1. You will look safer and feel safer when using positive body language. When you move with confidence and "project" positive vibes, you immediately feel more balanced and controlled.

2. Body language communication is contagious. We tend to imitate ourselves in the conversation. Did you notice that we seem to share the speed of speech, body movements, gestures, and facial expressions of the other person?

Isn't it surprising that we do this every day when we communicate? But we do that without even realizing it.

When you use positive body language, the other person is more likely to use positive body language (mirror), which makes the other person feel certain emotions (happier or safer in their decisions, etc.).

The opposite is true, so do not show any movement of body language, facial expressions, or gestures that have a negative tone or thought if you do not intend to do so.

We know that using positive body language improves everyone's mood. Look at a comedian who makes a crowd laugh with gestures, facial expressions, and body movements. Very often, the verbal message is fun, but body language simply reinforces the mood and reaction of the audience.

Here are some ways to communicate more effectively without the use of words:

1. Pay attention to positive clues that project you.

Whenever possible, make direct eye contact. Around 70% are acceptable in North America and the United Kingdom. In Japan, for example, the acceptable "observation rate" is closer to 50%, and in most Scandinavian countries, acceptable "observation rates" can reach up to 90%. Recognize that cultural differences are one of the three keys to interpreting body language.

b. Smile or relax your lips. Avoid tilting your lips or touching your face repeatedly. Nobody trusts someone who repeatedly touches their face when they speak.

c. Stand with an open attitude. Keep your legs and arms relaxed and loose, and try to stand aside, either at a slight angle to the other person or from the right eye to the right, when looking directly at the other person. It is more pleasant to look at the other person's left eye when speaking or listening.

d. Keep palms up and hands relaxed when talking. It is important that the open palm is revealed more frequently when gesturing while talking. This attracts the unconscious that you are not threatening.

Avoid nervous or twisted gestures, such as nail bumps or ring changes. This indicates a high degree of "internal dialogue" or "personal talk." It may indicate that you are anxious, restless and nervous or simply wish to continue.

2. When maintaining dialogue, pay close attention to the other person's body language. Watch for signs of negative body language or evidence that the client is bored. This may be that the other person is starting to look over his shoulder, playing with a zipper on a jacket, touching the keys and rubbing various items such as scarves, gloves, and hats. These are expressions of emotions and attitude.

3. Start subtly reproducing the other person's body language. If the client leans forward, he

must lean forward and show interest. If you have crossed your arms, bend your arms too, but point with your fingers and make sure they are separated. Once you're in the relationship, start leading. Try if you can lead. For example, if you eat with someone, drink your glass of water. If they also grab yours and follow you, you are in a good relationship now!

4. If you wish to give the conversation a more positive tone, slowly change your body language to make it more positive. Uncross your arms and legs, bow your head slightly while listening, and stretch your head while you speak. Nobody is serious when talking about business with an ironic head. (Note: When you go out or flirt, the head tilt works great and is extremely powerful!)

5. It is important to consider the following. Try not to change your body language (excessive body movement, touch your face, nervous knee movements, Figure 4) when you start talking, as this usually indicates that you are trying to take control of the conversation.

CHAPTER 13

HOW TO FIND A FAILURE TO SEE SIGNALS AND LINGUISTIC GESTURES

It is very important to have control over body language to lie successfully. Telephone, e-mail, or letter are the easiest ways for a person to settle. The mind may be able to write a credible and convincing story to support a lie, but the body will have great difficulty dealing with it.

Body language will betray the mind in many ways because the subconscious always acts independently and automatically during a spoken lie. This is why many amateur liars are easy to understand before they can even finish their story. No matter how convincing they sound, people will still be able to see those body language signals that contradict their words.

We have grouped these signals into categories ranging from those transmitted by facial expressions, which can be manipulated by the mind when practiced, to nervous systems that are more difficult to control and therefore more truthful.

Face the facts

Facial expression is considered the easiest to control because we always know what our faces are doing. Therefore, it is more difficult to say in the face if a person is lying or not. However, recent research has shown that, despite the high level of awareness of our facial movements, we still lack the mastery of visual expressions that our inner thoughts can reflect.

Before the brain can even send a message to what it wants to say, the eyes are already sending these small complementary signals. These tributes are considered reliable indicators of the fact that the statement contradicts the true basic sentiment.

If you look at someone straight in the eye, most people find it very difficult to lie. They will look down very quickly, look away, or look at you. These gestures are most commonly associated with the term "moving the eyes," which usually indicates confusion, dishonesty, and deception.

You must also remember that doubtful eyes do not always mean that someone is lying. He or she may be worried, pressured or simply confused about their opinions or feelings. However, you can be sure that this person is not currently able or willing to disclose their true feelings and thoughts and tries to hide this fact from you.

Through the teeth

Unfortunately, the phone has been a valuable tool since its inception, and many people lie to us. But fortunately, you can still recognize a liar with only your ears. If you carefully and accurately observe how words are spoken while ignoring the content, you may still be able to tell the truth from a lie.

Recent research has shown that the voice becomes less resonant when lying. If we hold back to express ourselves truthfully, the normal voice becomes flatter, loses depth, and becomes more monotonous.

Another fact is that people actually talk less when they lie and tend to make more mistakes in their speech. Unless they are well-trained speakers (e.g. salesmen, lawyers, politicians), they are more likely to stutter or hesitate when they speak.

Somewhere above the mouth

Children often cover their entire mouth when they lie, as if they wanted to hide the source of dishonesty. This original childhood gesture is also one of the most commonly used adult gestures for lying.

When a person lies, the brain unconsciously commands to suppress it

untruthful words that are said. The thumb is pressed against the cheek while the hand is used to cover the mouth. Occasionally, some people's gestures are just a few fingers on the mouth or even a tight fist, but the message remains very similar.

On the contrary, if someone does it while you talk, they may have difficulty believing you.

Touch Pinocchio's nose

When a person does not tell the truth, he rubs himself, caresses and scratches his nose more often than someone who is honest and direct. One explanation is simply that the nose is just above the mouth, and when the negative thoughts of deception enter the mind, the unconscious movement of the hand to cover the mouth is diverted to the nose.

Another ingenious reason is that lying increases tension and that tension causes a real physical itch in the nose. Therefore, the scratching of the nose can actually only be used to calm the itching sensation. However, there is a noticeable difference, since the true itch in a person's nose is usually satisfied by a more obvious rubbing movement, as opposed to a light touch or a touching nasal gesture that doubts itself.

Just like the hand on the mouth, it can be used both by the speaker to hide his own illusion and by the listener who is suspicious of what he is talking about.

Don't see an illusion, don't feel doubt

Rubbing or touching the eye area is a very strong indication of doubts and fraud. This gesture is the unconscious way in which the person tries not to look directly into the eyes or face of the person who is lying to him.

When a woman is lying, she usually rubs herself gently under the eye with a small and light gesture. This is because he prefers to avoid blurring the make-up, or it could just be the kind gesture of a typical woman since she grew up in a feminine environment.

Compared to a woman, a man usually rubs his eyes with a stronger gesture. However, when the deception is enormous, men and women share a similar gesture of avoiding the listener's gaze by looking at the floor or ceiling.

Undoubtedly coming to the side of the ear, rubbing, twisting or pulling the ear lobe is a sign of insecurity or confusion which, when performed during the speech, signals a lack of confidence in what the speaker is saying. It also means that the listener is not convinced of the truth of what is said of you when it is performed elsewhere while you speak.

These gestures that touch the ears are actually the improvised, adult version that has emerged from the ears of young children who want to exclude the annoyance and reproach of their parents.

Honest feet and legs

When someone decides to lie about something during a conversation, they usually cross their arms or legs at the same time. It indicates early self-defense against imminent challenges.

Other common foot signals may include a constant touch of the foot and feet pointing towards the exit. These gestures indicate that the person wants to get out of the current situation and get out. Normally, when a person tries to get out of something, it leads to the creation of a small harmless lie, rather than telling the truth in situations where they don't want to go to work or perform a particular social function.

The honest attitude

The posture of a person who is lying is often rigid and controlled. The natural physical expression of the person is retained if he holds the truth.

Research confirms that people are less likely to touch you or sit very close to you if they are dishonest. There is also a high probability that they will push your whole body away from you to hide both their face and the truth.

Another language of attitude that clashes with the spoken word can be socially seen when someone pretends to agree with you. The fact is that this person is simply not convinced and refuses you and what you say.

The stressful signals

The stress signals of the autonomic nervous system are the most reliable indications or indicators of dishonesty and insincerity. Stress reactions such as sweating, pallor, and irregular breathing are difficult to hide or even false. The most common and reliable indicator of lying is a dry mouth. This reaction to stress makes the liar lick more often on the lips and swallows nervously at certain times. Occasionally there are more hawks than usual.

These reactions to stress are caused by someone's increased sense of fear when he is lying. Such obvious stress symptoms usually occur only in dramatic circumstances.

Put it all together

Judging by the body gestures described here, obfuscation is probably the best word of lies to define the main influence behind everyone.

It will take time and observation to acquire the ability to accurately interpret and distinguish the many types of gestures in a given situation.

Any blowing one's nose or pulling ears does not necessarily mean that someone is lying intentionally. These so-called deceptive gestures can also be initiated by someone who simply expresses doubts, insecurity, confusion, exaggeration, or concern.

The ability to determine the correct mood of a person's gestures is the true capacity for interpretation. This can be achieved by analyzing the other types of signals immediately before displaying these cited gestures and interpreting them in context.

It is also very important to consider which culture someone comes, what kind of personality, and in what real situation is the person. Some cultures may not be particularly expressive, while others are dramatically demonstrative. Always remember to look at the whole image and not just one or two separate signals.

The use of a person's body language to determine if he is lying must be done carefully. You should not simply use an indicator to express your opinion. There are a number of indicators to use, and you should be aware of the many possible signals of body language that liars can give if they are fraudulent.

Always remember that a liar's body movements can mean he is cheating, but not always. You don't want to call someone a liar if you don't. This is why it is important to gather as many indicators and suggestions as possible. It is possible to misunderstand someone and judge him wrongly a liar. He or she may be very shy or inferior and may feel guilty even if they are innocent.

You must carefully consider every situation in which a person has been before the present moment. Is there some sort of emotional carryover that makes you misinterpret?

Are there cultural factors that make this person dishonest? Be sure that it can be normal and honest in your company to behave as you currently are. You must also be especially careful not to have any personal prejudices or prejudices against this person that could make you want him to be guilty of lying.

Another important factor, and probably the most important, is your ability to read a person's body language to see if he is lying.

An individual body language can help determine if they are lying to you. These non-verbal signals are different and include many types of movements and gestures. These can be observed when asking questions about the truth you want to find out. Each indicator should be displayed with other clues provided by the body language of the matter. These indicators should not be used alone to determine if someone is lying to you.

Here are some things to watch out for when determining the credibility of the answers given by the topic.

1. The subject nods or shakes his head unevenly with respect to the question asked. For example, if you ask the subject a question that requires a yes or no answer and the subject answers no, but moves his head up and down, it could be the physical manifestation of a lie.

2. The subject places his hand near or above his mouth. This could be a liar's body language.

3. Avoiding physical contact with other people in their environment can be a sign of fraud. This becomes even clearer when the two people are in a close relationship and usually have physical contact.

4. The person suspected of lying puts an object between himself and the person asking the questions.

These are some of the possible indicators that can be derived from a person's body language. You must carefully evaluate these indicators and more to express an opinion. Deciding if someone is lying is a serious matter and must be done thoughtfully and discreetly.

CHAPTER 14

THE BODY LANGUAGE OF TRUST

The technology we see now has turned the whole world into a global village. Opportunities also come from abroad. To take advantage of these opportunities, you just need to trust yourself. Self-confident people often find it easier to be successful emotionally, financially and socially. Everyone can improve their self-esteem. First of all, you need to make a decision. Are you ready to work hard and really focused on improving your self-esteem and self-esteem? Do you think about what you want to achieve in life? How does it help you improve your self-esteem to reach your goals?

Can you really increase your self-esteem in ten minutes?

It looks like one of those ridiculous claims that each Admonitor would not allow the model to pass, but we pause for a moment before both the baby's and the bath's water are drained into the drain.

If you want to increase your self-esteem, start with your body language. Even a slight shift can make a big difference in the way you feel. If you inhale your shoulders a little deeper and put a slight spring in the horse, you will immediately notice the changes. When you sit down, don't cross your arms or legs.

Try these steps to increase your self-esteem and automatically increase self-confidence. Think of positive thoughts about yourself! Focus on your strengths, not your weaknesses. Realize that you are better at some things than at others. Set realistic goals. This means that the goals are not set too high or too low, but at a level that you know you can achieve. So you can always strive to be better than your goal. Appreciate achieving a goal and praise yourself if you did well.

Celebrate a party! Who told you it was wrong? Learn to openly express your thoughts, opinions, needs, and feelings without abusing the rights of others. Don't compare yourself with others, remember, you're ok as you are! Comparison is one of the first reasons for low self-esteem and depression. They think others are better than you. If you think so, you're probably right, but it's actually completely wrong. Practice positive body language. Become big, don't sink. If your body says "I can", everyone will believe you can.

A. negative self-image is an obstacle to the success that many people must overcome in order to pursue their desires effectively. A series of therapeutic approaches can be used to increase customer confidence. One of the studies shows that the most effective intervention is neurolinguistic programming, which helps a person to relate memories of past results with current feelings of self-confidence.

What can you say about a person's body language? Actually, actually. The way a person gets and communicates through his body language says a lot about his mood, his general feelings, and his self-esteem. The way a person walks can be self-confidence, sexual attractiveness, aggression or sadness and shame.

If you doubt these statements, take some time when you are in a group or observe some people who really notice body language and see what it transmits. Someone who walks with a straight head and straight shoulders usually looks safe and secure. Someone with drooping shoulders and a look at the ground seems sad and downcast.

If someone is confident, confident, and has some respect for himself, he attracts those who treat him with respect. If you project yourself as someone who deserves consideration, appreciation, and appreciation, people will come back. The way you physically present yourself plays an important role.

Think about your total body language and ask yourself what kind of message you project on yourself. What is your attitude, your expression? Are you smiling or frowning? Are you sitting or sinking in your seat or walking? Do you describe yourself as someone who demands respect and attention or who is committed and accessible or someone who is sad, depressed and worthless?

You might decide to take some time to really look at the body language of others and see how they behave. Notice how some sit upright and project self-confidence to others who don't. See how gestures and body language change when a person is flirting or in an informal environment. Study how this confident employee sits or sits in a meeting or holds this presentation.

Practice good body language at home. Sit even if you watch TV. Keep your chin up slightly to increase self-confidence. Imitate what you see in movies and on television when you see characters that are professional and confident and see how they stand up or sit or even walk.

When you try to understand the body language of self-esteem or no self-esteem, you have to understand that all this comes from a simple lack of self-confidence, and this can be traced to how the person has been raised and what kind of situations you are with they are compared when they were still children.

When you enter the mental arena of self-esteem, you must understand that no one can give exactly one reason why people always lose their self-confidence. Many shrinks in the head have many different ways to describe your general self-esteem. You need to focus more on this.

Considering the sum of the word trust, or even other terms like pride and human ability to deal with a fact, we find that most of the other ways of describing it actually exist, and although authority is a general term for many things it seems, we know that moves from one position to another.

For one, it is something that most other people do naturally or try to do. For this reason, the most important thing to discuss when trying to be certain is that it is something that is incorporated and incorporated into the anthropomorphic psyche. The simple thing is that everyone has the power to be safe, and here you have to find that certainty again and get them out of the chaos in your agreement and bring it to the public.

Self-confidence also means interpreting another mortal very well and responding to it. Safety concerns the opinion and the ability to think without a bit of uncertainty about one's abilities and the words that are expressed. You can't be your self-critical criticism because you're so focused on a loser you can't face. At the end of the debate, it is always the way you come out of yourself, and that intellectual expulsion is the skin you will wear when you pounce on the spots.

It is something that the subconscious of other people can see and recognize and, of course, above all, can respond. You have no idea how much trust and power go hand in hand and, if you are looking for power, you can do almost anything you want. This is the secret and the supreme power of trust. When you show it as your body language, you are more charismatic and able to deal with everything that hinders you. It also doesn't hurt when you actually try to take advantage of the dating game. There's nothing better than having the self-confidence to break someone else's ground, and in the end, it depends on how you use that power - responsibly or not?

What is body language and how does it relate to your attitude and self-esteem? As we know, people communicate with each other. If we communicate only 7% of the words we use in our communication, most of the communication takes place with body language, vocal tones, tone, movement, and gestures. Body language means voice, speed, walking, eye contact, how fast you move, shoulders, chest. The question that arises is why body language is so important because we communicate with others.

Many things are spoken of in body language, including a person's self-esteem. The lack of self-confidence can be evident in many ways, including posture.

The way you wear is posture. It is a basis for first impressions, which usually dictate the image of one person in the eyes of another. Primary imitation can be very useful. In interviews, a person is generally judged based on his gestures, body language, and posture.

Usually, a tall person represents an image of self-confidence. Having good posture is a quick and safe way to make a good impression.

Posture is a careful effort to align the body with the center of gravity of the body. Everyone can easily distinguish someone who has a negative attitude. A person with a retired position is a person who sits with his shoulders lowered, and his head bowed as if he were looking for a long lost coin.

There may be so many reasons for the poor attitude. A cause of bad posture can already be considered a social norm. Maturity is superficial to worsen posture by carrying heavy bags and briefcases to work. People who spend time at the computer usually develop poor posture.

How can we correct our attitude? We must remember that a correct attitude requires conscious commitment and dedication. Below are some suggestions we can use to correct our negative attitude.

- Whenever possible, we must use a chair that fits perfectly in the backrest.
- The handles and straps of bags and backpacks must be padded and wide, supporting the shoulders and the back.
- Try sleeping on the back or side instead of sleeping on the stomach.

You can often pretend to be more confident in your body language.

The good thing is that not only can you deceive others into seeing you as confident, trustworthy, and expert but also deceive your brain.

If you want to see the body language of trust in action, you just have to look at the most important politicians in the world like Barack Obama. He walks with authority and speaks like a man of authority. Whatever your political choices, I don't think it's denied. Another advantage of looking at the body language of executives around the world is that they have often been specially trained to behave that way and have learned to use the mannerisms of a successful person who studies them!

Some of the obvious body languages can be seen in British political leaders, for whom some positions appear to be well trained. Let me guide you through some of them.

There is the bouncer of an exclusive nightclub with his hands behind his back. Have you ever noticed how many of them are like this? You have your shoulders back, your head high and your back straight.

The other is what is called "winking fingers." Put them in front of you as if you were praying, but instead turn your fingers into a church steeple. Here's how you look at the topic you're talking about. You'll see a lot at the conference table, which is mainly made by men.

One more thing that comes to mind is the arms behind the head, resting on the back of the chair, feet on the table, one leg crossed on the other at the ankle. This is the utmost confidence because it is so informal. My best example of this was a meeting with the "people" of Madonna, in which all the men who had been very successful in their field competed with each other. - They tried to outdo each other with the best and most intimate stories of the Madonna and to use all the different languages they could put together in one session - Nevertheless, it fun to watch.

Need help with your self-esteem? The best help is usually to introduce people into your life who will support you completely and only to get the most out of you and suppress the junk you have learned, such as doubt, low self-esteem and lack of self-confidence. Why do you want to assert yourself as an authority to hypnotize someone?

People are programmed to trust experts and leaders by establishing themselves as an authority and increasing the chances of success of their hypnotic suggestions. People trust you and listen to you more. That's why it's so important, and it's the first thing you need to do to hypnotize someone in secret.

How do you affirm yourself as a leader?

When you try to apply secret hypnosis to someone, you can build leadership and power using the right body language. You have to take a certain pose to appear to your subject as a figure of authority.

Use eye contact regularly. Try to avoid that your eyes fall on the subject's nose.

The longer you can maintain eye contact, the more self-esteem you have. Unconsciously, people appreciate your self-esteem based on how long you maintain eye contact.

If you are a man and talk to a woman, make sure you keep your eyes above shoulder level. This will create a sense of depth in her.

If you are a woman who meets a man, your first look should be turned to him from head to toe, that makes him feel flattered.

To establish authority, better visual contact is better. But there's more.

Here are other things you should know about your body language:

Your shoulders, make sure you hold them and lift your chin. This upright posture will show you that you are able to control every situation. While maintaining this attitude, it is important that you feel good.

Use leadership gestures. Move your arms in large movements while you talk. When you are quiet and listening, keep your hands behind your back. This makes you look relaxed, and you don't want to show strength, and you will subconsciously express power! (reverse psychology).

Make the tone of your voice deep and resonant. Take a break to punctuate all the sentences and sentences and use a bow down for each sentence you say.

When you sit down, you're at the top of the table. Keep your hands still and never hold them close to your face or body and keep your feet on the ground.

Now you have some basic terms of body language that you can use whenever you practice secret hypnosis in someone. Starting today, apply these techniques to your daily life for greater persuasion.

With the right body language, you can move on to an easier way to guide a person's mind to where you want to go. This is the first thing you need to do to establish a relationship, but not the only one. This is just the tips of the iceberg.

Transform yourself into an authority and a power figure using the right body language to attract more attention from your subjects and simplify the relationship process else it will be difficult to get secret hypnosis.

CONLUSION

To obtain knowledge, one must study; but to get wisdom, one must pay attention.

It seems a pity that we cannot limit communication to the words themselves. Our hearts - the seat of our intention - often reveal us and our body language tells us when the other person is sharp enough to pick it up:

"The most important thing in communication is listening to what is not said."

~ Peter Drucker (1909-2005)

All types of gestures are expressions of our heart

- far below our consciousness - and will betray the lies we say through our words and actions without integrity.

When we engage with our mannerisms - looking away from people when we talk when we fold our arms during the conversation, we sit or lean forward, etc. - we can begin to understand what we really communicate, what others are aware of or not.

If we want to be reliable, serious, good friends or safe people, we should know the inconsistency between our words and body language. Our body language can teach us a lot about ourselves.

Indeed, we can recognize that God uses our body language as a means of talking to us, highlighting inconsistencies in morality - lying by the truth.

Respect for our body language is also a reason to understand the body language of others. When we fight with integrity, we can forgive the other person who is fighting with himself in the same way.

Perhaps we can consider it a blessing that God gave us our judge and our jury - not to judge us, but to teach us. Life is the learning field.

We all know that action speaks more than words. No wonder we give so much importance to body language. It makes no sense to explain the importance of body language because we know the power and importance of that language. Now the question is whether it can be improved. In that case, how and to what extent?

If you want to improve it in this case, first try to understand your body language so that you can improve it later. Talk to your mirror, yes, do it first and try to observe how your body behaves in different situations like when you talk to your boss or friends or girlfriends.

Try to see if your words blend well with the body or not. One more thing, never try to fake your body language, in the long run, it could put you in a soup. Deception can never last long. Even looking at the body language of different people will greatly help your cause. Watch the gesture and attitude of celebrities, whether you are a movie star, a politician or a sports star, and try to see how they behave in specific situations as if they were on sticky doors and when they were in a good mood. And analyze later and then take something from it, obviously in small pieces. But always remember that something does not completely imitate it and only assumes gestures or attitudes or movements that adapt to your personality. Do not confuse mannerism with body language. In other words, it improves your body language based on your personality.

Improving body language and imitating someone are two different things. You may have noticed people crossing their arms or legs as they speak. In general, this gesture is associated with a defense mechanism, i.e. it is in a defensive or protected position. Therefore, try to avoid this gesture in real life while you take it. Ask everyone the same way and make sure that everyone gives you that they are making eye contact while they take it. Yes, it's true, but just make sure you make eye contact and don't stare. The dividing line between eye contact and excessive eye contact is very thin, so be careful. Work on your smile and laugh because it speaks at length about your personality. Imagine with a smile and then be normal. Don't keep your smile on your face unless you think this is the best way for you. Since you are at the end of the day, you will be able to assess the situation better, but try to avoid it.

Trust is an interesting feature for men and women. Women look for confident men because trust in a man is extremely attractive. A confident man knows what he wants, and also a self-confident woman. Nobody likes been with an insecure, hesitant partner who needs constant reassurance because it's too boring. This is how body language comes into play. Our body language indicates our state of mind and reflects our personality.

When we discover that our eyes are attracted to a man or a woman and we cannot look away, we often wonder what distinguishes the person from hundreds of people. Many people are unable to identify what this effect has on them. It is usually the body language of this person that we seek unconsciously because it satisfies what we seek internally.

If someone is looking for a random attack, they will look for someone to do the same signs. When we want something serious, we tend to stay away from flirtatious people. However, we can often deduce what kind of person a person is by observing it for a few minutes. It is the body language of a person who sends these signals to his environment. For this reason, people sometimes realize too late that a close friend or colleague who has always been interested in them has decided not to follow them.

This is often due to the signals we send. We could inadvertently attract or move people. Someone who takes the time to learn more about the right signals and body language can attract and allow more people in their lives instead of driving them away. Here are some signs that indicate that a person is interested in you. If you show these signs, a person interested in you will conclude that you accept their interest.

- When one person approaches another, it is often a sign of non-verbal interest.

- A relaxed body language indicates interest. Therefore, make sure your arms and legs are relaxed when they are accompanied by someone you care about.

- Eye contact says a lot. If someone looks you in the eye, this can be interpreted as their interest. If someone looks away, show that they are not interested in meeting you or that someone else is interested.

- A shy or shy smile is the way a woman tells a man to be interested. A warm, open smile should also be seen as a positive sign of interest.

- If someone moves away from you, has a rigid and disinterested facial expression, the limbs are crossed and tense, they constantly look away and have no visual contact, all these signs can be interpreted as a lack of interest.

People who are interested in you will plan for you. Note his feet, body direction, knees, and so on. This applies to both sexes. When many hairs contract, smile and look shy, it shows that the person is interested. Search for your body language to see if you are sending closed, uninterested signals or if you are telling other people that you are reachable. Your body language says it all, so you need to know what you say.

Everything we do or say comes from what is happening in us. We often look for external answers to solve internal problems. As an expression of your inner state, body language is ultimately no different. Of course, we can do external things that internalize new habits within us, but we must first recognize that our beliefs influence our behavior, our actions, the words and the subtle things that we communicate beyond words.

Beliefs are forms of thought that influence the way we see the world and the way we think, talk, act, and behave in the world. These beliefs affect body language and shape the way you move. So, before starting to become a mechanical robot, our priority should be to reject all limiting beliefs.

Limiting beliefs are those that prevent us from living the life we want and the experiences we want. The sole purpose of a belief is to prove true. The only purpose of a limiting belief is to limit yourself to low standards. When I believe that women do not like me, they are afraid of me or reject me; my body language shows this belief in a way that reminds me of such negative reactions and strengthens the belief itself.

If we change our beliefs and put aside our limiting beliefs - e.g. "I am an unattractive person." "I'm not rich enough." "I'm not a good interlocutor." "People find me boring." Greater body structures: our body language also naturally changes, reflecting a new inner state and opening new doors in our relationships with women. Pay more attention to the positive things you like about yourself; your body language changes automatically.

I rarely think of my body language. However, I am very aware of my body and "in my body." Whether I am very fluid or very calm in my movements, what I really communicate under the outer expression is the inner richness of a strengthening self-image. Common creativity. I agree that I don't need someone's permission. I communicate that I am in touch with myself, with my sexuality and with her.

Ultimately, we want to be aware of our body language, but don't focus on it at the expense of more important things.

Each person has a personal and individual way of expressing a message. And when there are patterns and rules in a conversation that needs to be respected based on context, environment, and purpose, there are also different body language settings to support the spoken word.

Body language, commonly referred to as non-verbal communication, is a key element in communicating messages that complement and reinforce verbal communication. Our body language can say a lot more about us than words can ever say. We can express thoughts, feelings, moods, character, attitude and so on. Furthermore, a person's body language is sometimes more honest than the verbal one. You can lie with words, but most likely your body will betray you.

The body is like a cinema screen on which information is projected and displayed through gestures and imitations. Whether you are anxious, sad, happy, or excited, your body projects your feelings and shows the observers what is happening inside. If you also pay attention to the details and look closely at a person's body language, you can see much more than they say, for example:

People who feel insecure, threatened, or insecure tend to touch themselves to comfort or hold themselves back. Rubbing your forehead, crossing your arms and keeping your fingers in front of your mouth and rubbing them are typical gestures that offer comfort and protection.

People in good spirits often take a deep breath and aim outwards with open arms. For instance, if you look at a picture of a winning athlete, you will most likely notice an open position with your arms open and your head tilted back while your eyes and mouth are open in ecstasy.

People who feel depressed or depressed or even desperate generally reveal their thoughts and attitudes through their hesitant steps, bent head or lowered eyes. However, positive people reveal their thoughts and their attitude with an upright posture, an elastic step, and a positive look, with vivid eyes.

However, not all bent heads cause depression. Sometimes it just means that a person thinks, thinks about something, focuses on something or absorbs information. If someone is asked to imitate someone who is really thinking, they will most likely prove it by placing their hands on their fingertips with their heads tilted and peering.

When you see someone with their heads bowed and their hands crossed, it is obvious to everyone that they are angry or worried. The position of the hands is a comforting gesture;

These are just some examples of common gestures in certain situations, but in reality, there are thousands of physical reactions, imitations, and gestures that reflect with surprising precision what is happening inside. Body language expresses much more than you can express with words, and sometimes even more than you want to show. However, if you know how to use it to your advantage, body language can become a powerful tool for interpersonal communication

Do you often feel that when you meet new people, you have the psychic ability to read their mood? Even if someone says he is happy or interested, does he have a strange feeling that the opposite is true?

Most of us can easily tell if someone is anxious, happy, sad, or angry. This is because 50-75% of communication actually comes from our body language. When our body language does not agree with the words we say, people literally feel the sense of separation. This feeling often leaves people confused and confused even when they don't know why.

Understanding body language or "reading" people is also a great way to get ahead in your work environment. It is about paying attention to non-verbal behavior. The things you can collect include how a person stands up or sits down, what he does with his hands or arms and whether he looks you straight in the eye or not. For example, even if someone stares at you with steel eyes, it does not necessarily tell the whole story. By "reading" body language, you can see if they are only paying attention to what they are saying, or if they are angry or disinterested.

Body language, which suggests that a person listens carefully, usually contains physical signals such as leaning forward or opening hands or arms. Attentive people can nod or listen with a smile while listening. These movements will help you feel comfortable and welcome and encourage you to continue the conversation.

On the other hand, if a person performs larger and more far-reaching movements, it may indicate that this particular person has a strong need for power. As a result, you may be surprised by their behavior and feel less comfortable or welcome in their presence.

There are other signs that a person is confused, disinterested, uncomfortable, or bored. You can see the tension in someone's forehead; Eye contact may not be uniform and, in fact, the person's eyes often shift from one thing to another. You can also see how his lips are joined, often suggesting impatience or confusion. Bored talking people can inadvertently tap their fingers on a desk, stir their feet, chew a pen or get off the chair. These movements show that he feels trapped and wants to escape at the first possible opportunity.

Believe it or not, understanding how people interact with their personal space can also help them understand their own. For example, take a moment to study a colleague's work area quickly. Is the area clean, large or small? Where are the chairs and the desk? How did you try to personalize your workplace? These territorial signals help you understand what kind of communicator the individual is and why you feel welcome in your environment.

At the same time, it is advisable to pay attention to one's body language. How do you signal to be happy or sad? How do you welcome the people who come to you and talk to you? How do you signal to be friendly and open to new relationships? People who understand their use of body language can use their non-verbal signals more effectively to their advantage.

It is sometimes said that the value of understanding non-verbal body language is worth more than a thousand words; in fact, it could also be more important than what is actually said. It does not take long to notice that this is a communication skill you can't do without!

What effect do my words/actions have and how can I judge them? Many people live their daily lives, both at work and at home, when they talk to other people and don't know exactly what effects their words or actions have on the other person. But the words and actions we use every day can do a lot to influence others around us.

"What's wrong with him/her or everything I said was ...?

Or how about, "I really don't know what I did, but he looks angry ...

Like how many times have you heard those phrases

Taking the time to study, a person's face reveals many emotions and feelings. If you are looking for signs, you can easily adapt your words and actions to the skills and techniques described in the previous articles to make a positive and lasting impression on others around us.

Try it and observe the telltale signs that betray a person's most intimate feelings.

Perhaps it is an imperceptible tightening around the eyes or the mouth if you think you explain something patiently.

A firming of the skin or perhaps even a color change from dark to light or vice versa.

Look at his body language, what does it tell you?

Are their shoulders straight, their heads tilted uneasily to the side, pulling their feet, maybe crossing their legs, their bodies leaning away from you and trying to distance themselves?

Do you feel good or bad in your area, and how can you say what to look for?

What is your breath, is it deep, shallow, fast, or slow?

Are your lips tense?

You talk and act the way you want it, and if you do not, you think, why could it be?

Many people respond to the signal or message that they can unconsciously send in their body language. For example, if you feel tense, tense, or nervous, pass that feeling on to the other person who "reflects" you, provided it is "hostile" when the emotions or feelings really come from you. The first thing you do is to check yourself and your speech patterns if you're using the right modality. To make that person happy, what kind of body language you use too close, too far?

Take the time to see how they react with other people in the office or at home, and pay particular attention to their language and body language as they will give you important clues about what makes them happy or unhappy.

Do you observe how they interact with the people they like, as well as with people they do not like and see if you can detect behavioral differences?

Her words are consistent with her actions. What do they really say and feel?

We often only notice in life when someone is angry when he starts to cry. We rely too much on people verbally telling us how they feel, rather than using our eyes and ears.

We do not want to know if a person is mad at us by hitting his nose, and we certainly do not want to "hallucinate" all sorts of ways with a contraction of the eyebrows.

If you want to be a really effective communicator, this is a lesson you cannot afford not to learn!

Do not go yet; One last thing to do

If you enjoyed this book or found it useful, I'd be very grateful if you'd post a short review on it. Your support really does make a difference and I read all the reviews personally so I can get your feedback and make this book even better.

Thanks again for your support!